Current
CONTROVERSIES

Sustainable
Consumption

Other Books in the Current Controversies Series

Agriculture
Attacks on Science
Domestic vs. Offshore Manufacturing
Fossil Fuel Industries and the Green Economy
The Gig Economy
Hate Groups
Holocaust Deniers and Conspiracy Theorists
Immigration, Asylum, and Sanctuary Cities
The Internet of Things
Libertarians, Socialists, and Other Third Parties
Nativism, Nationalism, and Patriotism

Sustainable Consumption

**Bridey Heing and
Erica Grove, Book Editors**

GREENHAVEN
PUBLISHING

Published in 2022 by Greenhaven Publishing, LLC
353 3rd Avenue, Suite 255, New York, NY 10010

Copyright © 2022 by Greenhaven Publishing, LLC

First Edition

Articles in Greenhaven Publishing anthologies are often edited for length to meet page
requirements. In addition, original titles of these works are changed to clearly present
the main thesis and to explicitly indicate the author's opinion. Every effort is made to
ensure that Greenhaven Publishing accurately reflects the original intent of the authors.
Every effort has been made to trace the owners of the copyrighted material.

Cover image: Roman Mikhailiuk/Shutterstock.com.

Library of Congress Cataloging-in-Publication Data

Names: Heing, Bridey, editor. | Grove, Erica M., editor.
Title: Sustainable consumption / Bridey Heing and Erica Grove, book
  editors.
Description: First edition. | New York, NY : Greenhaven Publishing, 2022. |
  Series: Current controversies | Includes bibliographical references and
index. | Audience: Ages 15+ | Audience: Grades 10–12 | Summary: "Diverse viewpoints
examine the role individual consumption plays in climate change, how companies have
attempted to become more sustainable, and if it is even possible to change consumption
practices enough to meaningfully impact climate change."— Provided by publisher.
Identifiers: LCCN 2020049079 | ISBN 9781534507821 (library binding) | ISBN
  9781534507807 (paperback) | ISBN 9781534507838 (ebook)
Subjects: LCSH: Sustainable living. | Consumption (Economics) |
  Sustainability—Economic aspects.
Classification: LCC GE196 .S865 2022 | DDC 338.9/27—dc23
LC record available at https://lccn.loc.gov/2020049079

Manufactured in the United States of America

Website: http://greenhavenpublishing.com

Foreword **11**

Introduction **14**

Chapter 1: Do Individual Consumption Choices Impact the Environment?

Overview: Natural and Human Factors Affect the
Environment **19**

What's Your Impact

Examining the main sources of carbon dioxide emissions shows that
both natural and human activity can change the environment.

**Yes: Individual Consumption Choices Drive the
Economy and Can Encourage Sustainable Practices**

Individual Household Practices Have a Substantial
Impact on Consumption **29**

Nancy Bazilchuk

Consumers are responsible for over 60 percent of greenhouse gas
emissions and 80 percent of the world's water use. Certain household
changes in consumption could significantly impact the environment.

Urban Residents Can Help Curb Climate Change by
Buying Less Stuff **34**

Alejandra Borunda

Key changes in consumption practices among urban residents can
help reduce their environmental impact.

Individual Consumption Choices Drive Societal Change **38**

Steve Westlake

The debate over whether individual actions or collective actions
have a greater impact is a false dichotomy. Individuals are part of the
collective solution.

Understanding Which Activities Have a Greater
Environmental Impact Can Help Reduce Consumption **41**

Morteza Taiebat and Ming Xu

Wealthier consumers have a larger carbon footprint, indicating that
consuming more has a greater environmental impact.

No: Individuals Are Limited in Their Ability to Positively Impact the Environment Because Corporations Hold the Power

Government Must Do More to Address Climate Change   **45**

Anders Levermann

Personal choices alone cannot solve the climate crisis. Governments and corporations need to do more to reduce carbon emissions.

Corporations Have the Biggest Impact on Climate Change **48**

Joshua Axelrod

Corporations must work to report emissions, use more recycled materials in manufacturing, and reduce emissions they generate.

Just 100 Companies Are to Blame for Over 70 Percent of Greenhouse Gas Emissions   **53**

Tess Riley

Because of the outsize influence companies have on global emissions, they must prioritize investing in renewable energy and resources and reducing their carbon emissions.

Blaming Individuals for Climate Change Is Inaccurate but Convenient for Corporations   **60**

Morten Fibieger Byskov

It is misguided to focus on how individuals can change their habits to address climate change, since they are statistically blameless.

Sustainability Will Not Be Possible Until Governments Stop Prioritizing Economic Growth   **63**

Federico Demaria

Policies that focus on growth for growth's sake ignore the fact that material resources are finite, standing in the way of sustainability on a broad scale.

Chapter 2: Have Companies Effectively Adopted Sustainable Practices?

Overview: Elements of Sustainable Business Development **68**

Fibre2Fashion

Today it benefits companies to have sustainability-oriented practices and goals.

Yes: It Is Beneficial for Companies to Focus on Sustainability, and Corporations Are Taking Note

Major Companies Are Adopting Sustainable Practices   **73**

Jo Confino

A number of notable corporations—including Ford, Starbucks, Walmart, and Nike—are working to become more sustainable.

Top Companies Are Motivated to Go Green   **78**

Rinkesh Kukreja

This viewpoint examines how seventeen companies are working to lead the pack in sustainability.

Sustainability Gives Businesses a Competitive Edge   **84**

Knut Haanaes

Expectations for corporate responsibility have grown over the years, so businesses need to focus on sustainability in order to stand out among the competition.

No: Currently, Most Companies Do Not Prioritize Sustainability

Companies Are Not Doing Enough to Prevent Climate Change   **90**

Alison Moodie

Companies need to work on setting long-term goals to reduce emissions immediately to effectively help curb climate change.

Companies Are More Focused on Short-Term Profitability than Long-Term Environmental Impacts   **93**

Andrew Winston

Most companies do not consider climate change a risk to their businesses and are largely unmotivated to take the drastic action needed to reduce their impact on the environment.

New Corporate Leadership Is Necessary for Businesses to Go Green   **96**

David Broadstock

Environmental sustainability and economic sustainability can go hand-in-hand if the next generation of corporate leaders chooses to prioritize green practices.

Chapter 3: Should Consumption and Production Be Regulated?

Overview: International Efforts to Support Sustainable Consumption and Production **100**

United Nations Environment Programme

International cooperation is necessary because of how many stakeholders are involved in implementing sustainable practices on a broad scale.

Yes: Regulation Is Necessary to Successfully Implement Sustainable Policies

The Government Is Responsible for Ecological Conservation **104**

Food and Agriculture Organization of the United Nations

The government—regional, state, or national—has the means to assess the state of natural resources and the ability to implement policies to protect these resources.

Enforcement of International Environmental Protection Laws Must Be Improved **115**

United Nations Environment Programme

International aid and cooperation have resulted in over 1,100 environmental agreements between countries since 1972. This is the first step to facilitating sustainable practices on an international scale.

Failure to Protect the Environment Will Have Negative Economic and Health Effects **118**

Ryan Nunn, Jimmy O'Donnell, Jay Shambaugh, Lawrence H. Goulder, Charles D. Kolstad, and Xianling Long

Renewable energy is becoming increasingly affordable. A wide range of approaches to emissions abatement are worth consideration.

No: Regulation Is Too Costly to Businesses and Consumers

Self-Regulation Can Be Good for Companies and Consumers **135**

Scott Shackelford

Businesses can encourage trust in their self-governance by turning to peers and industry groups to help set standards and ensure they are enforced.

Overregulation Stifles Growth and Innovation   **140**

Lalit Bhasin

Government policies that focus on helping businesses grow have a number of positive economic impacts. Regulation can stifle economic success.

Consumers Pay a High Price for Regulation   **143**

Sam Batkins

Even though the potential positive environmental impacts of regulations often get the most attention, it is worth keeping in mind that these regulations can also cause significant price increases for consumers.

Chapter 4: Is It Possible for Consumption to Become More Sustainable?

Overview: Convenient Consumption Isn't Always Sustainable Consumption   **151**

Science History Institute

Plastics have become a critical part of modern life, but they bring with them a number of environmental and health concerns.

Yes: It Is Possible to Find More Sustainable Forms of Consumption

Plastics and Disposability Are the Primary Problems with Consumption   **156**

Susan Strasser

The growth of the plastics industry led to a consumer culture centered on disposability. Through reusing more goods and disposing less, it is possible to consume more sustainably.

Sustainable Development Depends on Environmental, Social, and Economic Factors   **161**

Matthew Mason

In order to promote economic and social development, quality of life must be maintained and, when possible, improved. Consumption is necessary to enable this.

Manufacturing Is Becoming More Sustainable   **168**

Joseph Rauch

Partially due to consumers' interest in supporting sustainable businesses, manufacturers are working to find ways to lessen their environmental impact.

No: Consumption Can Never Be Truly Sustainable

Consuming Less Would Create a More Fulfilling
Way of Life   **173**

Samuel Alexander

"Degrowth" is the only sustainable option. However, degrowth would need to be a coordinated effort that ensures everyone has enough to comfortably survive.

Economic Growth Stands in the Way of Sustainability   **179**

Juliette Legendre

It is possible to ensure the well-being of citizens in an environmentally sustainable way, which challenges traditional ways of thinking about the economy.

Consume Less to Protect the Planet's Finite Resources   **183**

Sophie Perryer

Proponents of the degrowth movement argue that endless production, consumption, and economic growth is not sustainable in a world of finite resources.

Drastic Action Is Needed to Reduce the Impacts of Climate
Change   **188**

United Nations Development Programme

At the moment, the world is not on track to meet the sustainable development goals set in place by the United Nations. Reducing greenhouse gas emissions on a global scale is necessary to mitigate the effects of climate change.

Organizations to Contact   **190**

Bibliography   **194**

Index   **197**

Foreword

Controversy" is a word that has an undeniably unpleasant connotation. It carries a definite negative charge. Controversy can spoil family gatherings, spread a chill around classroom and campus discussion, inflame public discourse, open raw civic wounds, and lead to the ouster of public officials. We often feel that controversy is almost akin to bad manners, a rude and shocking eruption of that which must not be spoken or thought of in polite, tightly guarded society. To avoid controversy, to quell controversy, is often seen as a public good, a victory for etiquette, perhaps even a moral or ethical imperative.

Yet the studious, deliberate avoidance of controversy is also a whitewashing, a denial, a death threat to democracy. It is a false sterilizing and sanitizing and superficial ordering of the messy, ragged, chaotic, at times ugly processes by which a healthy democracy identifies and confronts challenges, engages in passionate debate about appropriate approaches and solutions, and arrives at something like a consensus and a broadly accepted and supported way forward. Controversy is the megaphone, the speaker's corner, the public square through which the citizenry finds and uses its voice. Controversy is the life's blood of our democracy and absolutely essential to the vibrant health of our society.

Our present age is certainly no stranger to controversy. We are consumed by fierce debates about technology, privacy, political correctness, poverty, violence, crime and policing, guns, immigration, civil and human rights, terrorism, militarism, environmental protection, and gender and racial equality. Loudly competing voices are raised every day, shouting opposing opinions, putting forth competing agendas, and summoning starkly different visions of a utopian or dystopian future. Often these voices attempt to shout the others down; there is precious little listening and considering among the cacophonous din. Yet listening and considering, too, are essential to the health of a democracy. If controversy is democracy's lusty lifeblood, respectful listening and careful thought are its higher faculties, its brain, its conscience.

Current Controversies does not shy away from or attempt to hush the loudly competing voices. It seeks to provide readers with as wide and representative as possible a range of articulate voices on any given controversy of the day, separates each one out to allow it to be heard clearly and fairly, and encourages careful listening to each of these well-crafted, thoughtfully expressed opinions, supplied by some of today's leading academics, thinkers, analysts, politicians, policy makers, economists, activists, change agents, and advocates. Only after listening to a wide range of opinions on an issue, evaluating the strengths and weaknesses of each argument, assessing how well the facts and available evidence mesh with the stated opinions and conclusions, and thoughtfully and critically examining one's own beliefs and conscience can the reader begin to arrive at his or her own conclusions and articulate his or her own stance on the spotlighted controversy.

This process is facilitated and supported in each Current Controversies volume by an introduction and chapter overviews that provide readers with the essential context they need to begin engaging with the spotlighted controversies, with the debates surrounding them, and with their own perhaps shifting or nascent opinions on them. Chapters are organized around several key questions that are answered with diverse opinions representing all points on the political spectrum. In its content, organization, and methodology, readers are encouraged to determine the authors' point of view and purpose, interrogate and analyze the various arguments and their rhetoric and structure, evaluate the arguments' strengths and weaknesses, test their claims against available facts and evidence, judge the validity of the reasoning, and bring into clearer, sharper focus the reader's own beliefs and conclusions and how they may differ from or align with those in the collection or those of classmates.

Research has shown that reading comprehension skills improve dramatically when students are provided with compelling, intriguing, and relevant "discussable" texts. The subject matter of these collections could not be more compelling, intriguing, or urgently relevant to today's students and the world they are poised to inherit. The anthologized articles also provide the basis for stimulating, lively, and passionate classroom debates. Students who are compelled to anticipate objections to their own argument and identify the flaws in those of an opponent read more carefully, think more critically, and steep themselves in relevant context, facts, and information more thoroughly. In short, using discussable text of the kind provided by every single volume in the Current Controversies series encourages close reading, facilitates reading comprehension, fosters research, strengthens critical thinking, and greatly enlivens and energizes classroom discussion and participation. The entire learning process is deepened, extended, and strengthened.

If we are to foster a knowledgeable, responsible, active, and engaged citizenry, we must provide readers with the intellectual, interpretive, and critical-thinking tools and experience necessary to make sense of the world around them and of the all-important debates and arguments that inform it. We must encourage them not to run away from or attempt to quell controversy but to embrace it in a responsible, conscientious, and thoughtful way, to sharpen and strengthen their own informed opinions by listening to and critically analyzing those of others. This series encourages respectful engagement with and analysis of current controversies and competing opinions and fosters a resulting increase in the strength and rigor of one's own opinions and stances. As such, it helps readers assume their rightful place in the public square and provides them with the skills necessary to uphold their awesome responsibility—guaranteeing the continued and future health of a vital, vibrant, and free democracy.

Introduction

> *"The human race is challenged more than ever before to demonstrate our mastery, not over nature but of ourselves."*
>
> —*Rachel Carson, marine biologist, conservationist, and author*

G iven the current circumstances of life on Earth, one cannot help but feel anxious when considering its future. Environmental catastrophes like wildfires, droughts, hurricanes, and floods have become increasingly common. Since 1981, combined land and ocean temperatures have increased at a rate of 0.32°F (0.18°C) per year, which is a contributing factor in these extreme weather events. Immense islands made of discarded plastic are forming in oceans from the approximately 8 million tons of plastic that float out to sea each year. It has become increasingly clear that the resources the earth has to offer are finite, and that its climate and ecology are in a delicate balance that could easily be pushed over the edge.

However, even though there is a growing awareness of the impact humanity has on the environment and the need to preserve the resources we have, consumption and waste are still massive problems. In 2017 alone, around 139.6 million tons—or 4.51 pounds per person per day—of solid waste was landfilled in the US, with food waste accounting for 22 percent, plastics for 19 percent, paper and cardboard for around 13 percent, and rubber, leather, and textiles for over 11 percent. Additionally, even though greenhouse gas emissions are commonly recognized as a major cause of climate change, global carbon emissions reached an all-time high in 2019. Countries struggle to reach the international climate goals laid out in the Paris Agreement of 2016, which is focused on reducing emissions and mitigating the effects of climate change.

Despite these ominous figures—or perhaps because of them—it is more important than ever for consumers, corporations, and governments to cooperate in finding ways to promote ecological sustainability. Sustainability refers to practices that avoid depleting natural resources and help maintain the biosphere. However, who ultimately holds the power in addressing this issue is widely debated. Many consumers make a meaningful effort to recycle their waste whenever possible, which has caused recycling rates to increase from 6 percent of waste generated in the US in 1960 to over 35 percent of total waste in 2017. Recycling has been heralded as an opportunity for consumers to make a positive impact on the environment, but in reality the results of these programs have been mixed. Since 2003, the US has met or exceeded a 63 percent recycling rate for paper, and a number of commonly-used metals have recycling rates that exceed 50 percent, with steel leading the pack at 88 percent. However, despite marketing efforts to assure consumers that plastics are easily recyclable, as of 2017 only 8.4 percent of plastics were recycled in the US. Furthermore, even when plastics are collected for recycling, a significant amount of it still ends up in landfills because of the cost and difficulty of recycling it, along with China's refusal to continue purchasing recycled plastic from the US. Though consumers can help work towards greater sustainability through recycling, it is clear that this is not a perfect solution.

So what can be done to more effectively promote sustainability? There are numerous ways in which corporations are attempting to go green. Clothing companies attempt to be more sustainable through reducing water usage in production, using more recycled and decomposable materials, utilizing more natural organic fibers, and reducing the use of hazardous chemicals. Grocery stores like

Walmart and Trader Joe's help reduce their environmental impact by working with more suppliers that practice sustainability and are Fair Trade certified, reducing the use of plastic bags and other single-use plastics, making stores energy efficient, and using fuel-efficient transportation for their supplies. Electric and hybrid cars—which combine electric and gasoline power—have become increasingly popular, and major manufacturers like Chevrolet, Ford, and Nissan have joined Tesla in producing more efficient vehicles. However, "greenwashing"—deceptive marketing strategies that make products and companies seem more environmentally friendly than they actually are—is a major issue. Consumers are increasingly interested in buying green products, but it can be expensive for companies to actually make the switch to sustainability. It is particularly difficult to tell if greenwashing is taking place because there are so many competing ecolabels found on products with widely differing standards for certification. Ultimately, it falls to consumers to determine which brands and ecolabels they can trust to be sustainable and whether they wish to support these businesses.

Ultimately, governments may have the most influence over sustainability. They have the power to force corporations and individuals to act more sustainably by reducing greenhouse gas emissions and waste. They can support more eco-friendly forms of public transportation and increased use of renewable energy. They can pass legislation that protects ecosystems, promotes recycling, and fights pollution. Ultimately, they have the authority to make sustainable policies law, just as France did in 2016 by passing a law that forbids grocery stores from throwing away edible food. While individuals and corporations may lack the motivation or influence to make a major environmental impact, politicians can use policymaking to enact change on a city-wide, national, or even global level.

The viewpoints presented in Current Controversies: Sustainable Consumption consider numerous differing perspectives on the ability of consumers, corporations, and governments to promote sustainable consumption practices. They examine the efforts that are currently being made to address sustainability and debate the efficacy of these efforts and proposed solutions. Ultimately, the authors contemplate whether it is possible for consumption to be sustainable at all, with some arguing that we should shift our focus to degrowth—the concept of consuming and producing less overall—and away from the prospect of sustainable growth. Readers will be empowered to form their own opinions about the potential of sustainable consumption and the possible means of achieving it.

CHAPTER 1

Do Individual Consumption Choices Impact the Environment?

Overview: Natural and Human Factors Affect the Environment

What's Your Impact

What's Your Impact is a nonprofit organization focused on empowering individuals to fight climate change. It examines the causes of climate change and encourages readers to take action in their own lives.

There are both natural and human sources of carbon dioxide emissions. Natural sources include decomposition, ocean release and respiration. Human sources come from activities like cement production, deforestation as well as the burning of fossil fuels like coal, oil and natural gas.

Due to human activities, the atmospheric concentration of carbon dioxide has been rising extensively since the Industrial Revolution and has now reached dangerous levels not seen in the last 3 million years. Human sources of carbon dioxide emissions are much smaller than natural emissions but they have upset the natural balance that existed for many thousands of years before the influence of humans.

This is because natural sinks remove around the same quantity of carbon dioxide from the atmosphere than are produced by natural sources. This had kept carbon dioxide levels balanced and in a safe range. But human sources of emissions have upset the natural balance by adding extra carbon dioxide to the atmosphere without removing any.

Carbon Dioxide Emissions: Human Sources

Since the Industrial Revolution, human sources of carbon dioxide emissions have been growing. Human activities such as the burning

"Main Sources of Carbon Dioxide Emissions," What's Your Impact. https://whatsyourimpact.org/greenhouse-gases/carbon-dioxide-emissions. Licensed under CC BY-SA 4.0.

of oil, coal and gas, as well as deforestation are the primary cause of the increased carbon dioxide concentrations in the atmosphere.

87 percent of all human-produced carbon dioxide emissions come from the burning of fossil fuels like coal, natural gas and oil. The remainder results from the clearing of forests and other land use changes (9%), as well as some industrial processes such as cement manufacturing (4%).

Fossil Fuel Combustion/Use

The largest human source of carbon dioxide emissions is from the combustion of fossil fuels. This produces 87% of human carbon dioxide emissions. Burning these fuels releases energy which is most commonly turned into heat, electricity or power for transportation. Some examples of where they are used are in power plants, cars, planes and industrial facilities. In 2011, fossil fuel use created 33.2 billion tonnes of carbon dioxide emissions worldwide.

The 3 types of fossil fuels that are used the most are coal, natural gas and oil. Coal is responsible for 43% of carbon dioxide emissions from fuel combustion, 36% is produced by oil and 20% from natural gas.

Coal is the most carbon intensive fossil fuel. For every tonne of coal burned, approximately 2.5 tonnes of CO_2 are produced. Of all the different types of fossil fuels, coal produces the most carbon dioxide. Because of this and it's high rate of use, coal is the largest fossil fuel source of carbon dioxide emissions. Coal represents one-third of fossil fuels' share of world total primary energy supply but is responsible for 43% of carbon dioxide emissions from fossil fuel use.

Anything involving fossil fuels has a carbon dioxide emission ticket attached. So for example, burning these fuels releases energy but carbon dioxide also gets produced as a byproduct. This is because almost all the carbon that is stored in fossil fuels gets transformed to carbon dioxide during this process.

The three main economic sectors that use fossil fuels are: electricity/heat, transportation and industry. The first two sectors, electricity/heat and transportation, produced nearly two-thirds of global carbon dioxide emissions in 2010.

Electricity/Heat Sector

Electricity and heat generation is the economic sector that produces the largest amount of man-made carbon dioxide emissions. This sector produced 41% of fossil fuel related carbon dioxide emissions in 2010. Around the world, this sector relies heavily on coal, the most carbon-intensive of fossil fuels, explaining this sector giant carbon footprint.

Almost all industrialized nations get the majority of their electricity from the combustion of fossil fuels (around 60-90%). Only Canada and France are the exception. Depending on the energy mix of your local power company you probably will find that the electricity that you use at home and at work has a considerable impact on greenhouse gas emissions.

Below is a chart for percentage of electrical energy produced by fossil fuel combustion for major industrialized nations.

Electrical Energy Produced by Fossil Fuel Combustion (Billion Kilowatthours)

G8 NATION	FOSSIL FUEL COMBUSTION	TOTAL	%
Canada	136.31	622.98	21.9%
France	44.65	532.57	8.4%
Germany	340.38	567.33	60.0%
Italy	286.35	201.7	70.4%
Japan	759.93	1,031.22	73.7%
Russia	668.26	996.82	67.0%
United Kingdom	244.5	342.48	71.4%
United States	2,788.87	4,100.14	68.0%

SOURCE: International Energy Statistics Database (2011), Energy Information Administration

The industrial, residential and commercial sectors are the main users of electricity covering 92% of usage. Industry is the largest consumer of the three because certain manufacturing processes are very energy intensive. Specifically, the production of chemicals, iron/steel, cement, aluminum as well as pulp and paper account for the great majority of industrial electricity use. The residential and commercial sectors are also heavily reliant on electricity for meeting their energy needs, particularly for lighting, heating, air conditioning and appliances.

Transportation Sector

The transportation sector is the second largest source of anthropogenic carbon dioxide emissions. Transporting goods and people around the world produced 22% of fossil fuel related carbon dioxide emissions in 2010. This sector is very energy intensive and it uses petroleum based fuels (gasoline, diesel, kerosene, etc.) almost exclusively to meet those needs. Since the 1990s, transport related emissions have grown rapidly, increasing by 45% in less than 2 decades.

Road transport accounts for 72% of this sector's carbon dioxide emissions. Automobiles, freight and light-duty trucks are the main sources of emissions for the whole transport sector and emissions from these three have steadily grown since 1990. Apart from road vehicles, the other important sources of emissions for this sector are marine shipping and global aviation.

Marine shipping produces 14% of all transport carbon dioxide emissions. While there are a lot less ships than road vehicles used in the transportation sector, ships burn the dirtiest fuel on the market, a fuel that is so unrefined that it can be solid enough to be walked across at room temperature. Because of this, marine shipping is responsible for over 1 billion tonnes of carbon dioxide emissions. This is more than the annual emissions of several industrialized countries (Germany, South Korea, Canada, UK, etc.) and this sector continues to grow rapidly.

Global aviation accounts for 11% of all transport carbon dioxide emissions. International flights create about 62% of these emissions with domestic flights representing the remaining 38%. Over the last 10 years, aviation has been one of the fastest growing sources of carbon dioxide emissions. Aviation is also the most carbon-intensive form of transportation, so it's growth comes with a heavy impact on climate change.

Emissions caused by the transportation of people and goods has grown so rapidly that it has surpassed emissions from the industrial sector, which has had a huge impact on climate change. This trend started in the 1990's and has continued ever since causing an increase in indirect emissions.

The emissions caused by the transportation of goods are examples of indirect emissions since the consumer has no direct control of the distance between the factory and the store. The emissions caused by people traveling (by car, plane, train, etc...) are examples of direct emissions since people can chose where they are going and by what method.

Since the distance traveled by goods during production is continuing to grow, this is putting more pressure on the transportation industry to bridge the gap and ends up creating more indirect emissions. What's worse is that 99% of the carbon dioxide emissions caused by transportation of people and goods all over the world comes from the combustion of fossil fuels.

Industrial Sector

The industrial sector is the third largest source of man-made carbon dioxide emissions. This sector produced 20% of fossil fuel related carbon dioxide emissions in 2010. The industrial sector consists of manufacturing, construction, mining, and agriculture. Manufacturing is the largest of the 4 and can be broken down into 5 main categories: paper, food, petroleum refineries, chemicals, and metal/mineral products. These categories account for the vast majority of the fossil fuel use and CO_2 emissions by this sector.

Manufacturing and industrial processes all combine to produce large amounts of each type of greenhouse gas but specifically large amounts of CO_2. This is because many manufacturing facilities directly use fossil fuels to create heat and steam needed at various stages of production. For example factories in the cement industry, have to heat up limestone to 1450°C to turn it into cement, which is done by burning fossil fuels to create the required heat.

Land Use Changes

Land use changes are a substantial source of carbon dioxide emissions globally, accounting for 9% of human carbon dioxide emissions and contributed 3.3 billion tonnes of carbon dioxide emissions in 2011. Land use changes are when the natural environment is converted into areas for human use like agricultural land or settlements. From 1850 to 2000, land use and land use change released an estimated 396-690 billion tonnes of carbon dioxide to the atmosphere, or about 28-40% of total anthropogenic carbon dioxide emissions.

Deforestation has been responsible for the great majority of these emissions. Deforestation is the permanent removal of standing forests and is the most important type of land use change because its impact on greenhouse gas emissions. Forests in many areas have been cleared for timber or burned for conversion to farms and pastures. When forested land is cleared, large quantities of greenhouse gases are released and this ends up increasing carbon dioxide levels in three different ways.

Trees act as a carbon sink. They remove carbon dioxide from the atmosphere via photosynthesis. When forests are cleared to create farms or pastures, trees are cut down and either burnt or left to rot, which adds carbon dioxide to the atmosphere.

Since deforestation reduces the amount of trees, this also reduces how much carbon dioxide can be removed by the Earth's forests. When deforestation is done to create new agricultural land, the crops that replace the trees also act as a carbon sink, but they are not as effective as forests. When trees are cut for lumber the wood is kept which locks the carbon in it but the carbon sink provided by forests is reduced because of the loss of trees.

Deforestation also causes serious changes in how carbon is stored in the soil. When forested land is cleared, soil disturbance and increased rates of decomposition in converted soils both create carbon dioxide emissions. This also increases soil erosion and nutrient leaching which further reduces the area's ability to act as a carbon sink.

Industrial Processes

There are many industrial processes that produce significant amounts of carbon dioxide emissions as a by product of chemical reactions needed in their production process. Industrial processes account for 4% of human carbon dioxide emissions and contributed 1.7 billion tonnes of carbon dioxide emissions in 2011.

Many industrial processes emit carbon dioxide directly through fossil fuel combustion as well indirectly through the use of electricity that is generated using fossil fuels. But there are four main types of industrial process that are a significant source of carbon dioxide emissions: the production and consumption of mineral products such as cement, the production of metals such as iron and steel, as well as the production of chemicals and petrochemical products.

Cement production produces the most amount of carbon dioxide amongst all industrial processes. To create the main ingredient in cement, calcium oxide, limestone is chemically transformed by heating it to very high temperatures. This process produces large quantities of carbon dioxide as a byproduct of the chemical reaction. So much so that making 1000 kg of cement produces nearly 900 kg of carbon dioxide.

Steel production is another industrial process that is an important source of carbon dioxide emissions. To create steel, iron is melted and refined to lower its carbon content. This process uses oxygen to combine with the carbon in iron which creates carbon dioxide. On average, 1.9 tonnes of CO_2 are emitted for every tonne of steel produced.

Fossil fuels are used to create chemicals and petrochemical products which leads to carbon dioxide emissions. The industrial production of ammonia and hydrogen most often use natural gas or other fossil fuels as a starting base, creating carbon dioxide in the process. Petrochemical products like plastics, solvents, and lubricants are created using petroleum. These products evaporate, dissolve, or wear out over time releasing even more carbon dioxide during the product's life.

Carbon Dioxide Emissions: Natural Sources

Apart from being created by human activities, carbon dioxide is also released into the atmosphere by natural processes. The Earth's oceans, soil, plants, animals and volcanoes are all natural sources of carbon dioxide emissions.

Human sources of carbon dioxide are much smaller than natural emissions but they upset the balance in the carbon cycle that existed before the Industrial Revolution. The amount of carbon dioxide produced by natural sources is completely offset by natural carbon sinks and has been for thousands of years. Before the influence of humans, carbon dioxide levels were quite steady because of this natural balance.

42.84 percent of all naturally produced carbon dioxide emissions come from ocean-atmosphere exchange. Other important natural sources include plant and animal respiration (28.56%) as well as soil respiration and decomposition (28.56%). A minor amount is also created by volcanic eruptions (0.03%).

Ocean-Atmosphere Exchange

The largest natural source of carbon dioxide emissions is from ocean-atmosphere exchange. This produces 42.84% of natural carbon dioxide emissions. The oceans contain dissolved carbon dioxide, which is released into the air at the sea surface.

Annually this process creates about 330 billion tonnes of carbon dioxide emissions.

Many molecules move between the ocean and the atmosphere through the process of diffusion, carbon dioxide is one of them. This movement is in both directions, so the oceans release carbon dioxide but they also absorb it. The effects of this movement can be seen quite easily, when water is left to sit in a glass for long enough, gases will be released and create air bubbles. Carbon dioxide is amongst the gases that are in the air bubbles.

Plant and Animal Respiration

An important natural source of carbon dioxide is plant and animal respiration, which accounts for 28.56% of natural emissions. Carbon dioxide is a byproduct of the chemical reaction that plants and animals use to produce the energy they need. Annually this process creates about 220 billion tonnes of carbon dioxide emissions.

Plants and animals use respiration to produce energy, which is used to fuel basic activities like movement and growth. The process uses oxygen to break down nutrients like sugars, proteins and fats. This releases energy that can be used by the organism but also creates water and carbon dioxide as byproducts.

Soil Respiration and Decomposition

Another important natural source of carbon dioxide is soil respiration and decomposition, which accounts for 28.56% of natural emissions. Many organisms that live in the Earth's soil use respiration to produce energy. Amongst them are decomposers who break down dead organic material. Both of these processes releases carbon dioxide as a byproduct. Annually these soil organisms create about 220 billion tonnes of carbon dioxide emissions.

Any respiration that occurs below-ground is considered soil respiration. Plant roots, bacteria, fungi and soil animals use respiration to create the energy they need to survive but this also produces carbon dioxide. Decomposers that work underground breaking down organic matter (like dead trees, leaves and animals) are also included in this. Carbon dioxide is regularly released during decomposition.

Volcanic Eruptions

A minor amount carbon dioxide is created by volcanic eruptions, which accounts for 0.03% of natural emissions. Volcanic eruptions release magma, ash, dust and gases from deep below the Earth's surface. One of the gases released is carbon dioxide. Annually this process creates about 0.15 to 0.26 billion tonnes of carbon dioxide emissions.

The most common volcanic gases are water vapor, carbon dioxide, and sulfur dioxide. Volcanic activity will cause magma to absorb these gases, while passing through the Earth's mantle and crust. During eruptions, the gases are then released into the atmosphere.

Individual Household Practices Have a Substantial Impact on Consumption

Nancy Bazilchuk

Nancy Bazilchuk is a Norway-based science and environmental writer. She has written for numerous magazines, newspapers, and trade publications, including Scientific American.com, Audubon, and the Norwegian University of Science and Technology's Norwegian SciTech News.

The world's workshop—China—surpassed the United States as the largest emitter of greenhouse gases on Earth in 2007. But if you consider that nearly all of the products that China produces, from iPhones to tee-shirts, are exported to the rest of the world, the picture looks very different.

"If you look at China's per capita consumption-based (environmental) footprint, it is small," says Diana Ivanova, a PhD candidate at Norwegian University of Science and Technology's (NTNU) Industrial Ecology Programme. "They produce a lot of products but they export them. It's different if you put the responsibility for those impacts on the consumer, as opposed to the producer."

That's exactly what Ivanova and her colleagues did when they looked at the environmental impact from a consumer perspective in 43 different countries and 5 rest-of-the-world regions. Their analysis, recently published in the Journal of Industrial Ecology, showed that consumers are responsible for more than 60 per cent of the globe's greenhouse gas emissions, and up to 80 per cent of the world's water use.

"We all like to put the blame on someone else, the government, or businesses," Ivanova says. "But between 60-80 per cent of the impacts on the planet come from household consumption. If we change our consumption habits, this would have a drastic effect on our environmental footprint as well."

The analysis allowed Ivanova and her colleagues to see that consumers are directly responsible for 20 per cent of all carbon impacts, which result from when people drive their cars and heat their homes.

But even more surprising is that four-fifths of the impacts that can be attributed to consumers are not direct impacts, like the fuel we burn when we drive our cars, but are what are called secondary impacts, or the environmental effects from actually producing the goods and products that we buy.

A good example of this, Ivanova says, is water use.

Cows, Not Showers

When you think about cutting your individual water use, you might think about using your dishwasher very efficiently, or taking shorter showers.

Those aren't bad ideas on their own, but if you look deeper, like the NTNU researchers did, you'll find that much of the water use on the planet is gulped up by producing the things that you buy.

Consider beef. Producing beef requires lots of water because cows eat grains that need water to grow. But because cows are relatively inefficient in converting grains into the meat that we eat, it takes on average about 15,415 litres of water to produce one kilo of beef.

Dairy products require similarly large amounts of water to produce.

When a group of Dutch researchers looked at the difference in producing a litre of soy milk with soybeans grown in Belgium compared to producing a litre of cow's milk, they found it took 297 litres of water to make the soy milk (with 62 per cent of that from actually growing the soybeans) versus a global average of 1050 litres of water to produce a litre of cow's milk.

Processed foods, like that frozen pizza you bought for dinner last night, are also disproportionately high in water consumption,

Ivanova said. Making processed foods requires energy, materials and water to grow the raw materials, ship them to the processor, produce the processed food items and then package the final product.

This is particularly bad news when it comes to chocolate, which is one of the most water-intensive products we can buy. It takes a shocking 17,000 litres to produce a kilo of chocolate.

Richer Countries, Larger Impacts

The researchers also looked at environmental impacts on a per-capita, country-by-country basis.

While the information is sometimes surprising—Luxembourg has a per capita carbon footprint that is nearly the same as the United States—it mostly follows a predictable pattern. The richer a country is, the more its inhabitants consume. The more an individual consumes, the bigger that person's impact on the planet.

But the differences between individual countries are extremely high, Ivanova said.

"The countries with the highest consumption have about a 5.5 times higher environmental impact over the world average," she said.

The United States is the overall worst performer when it comes to per capita greenhouse gas emissions, with a per capita carbon footprint of 18.6 tonnes CO_2 equivalent, the unit used by researchers to express the sum of the impacts of different greenhouse gases, such as carbon dioxide, methane, nitrous oxide and sulphur hexafluoride.

The US was followed closely by Luxembourg, with 18.5 tonnes CO_2 equivalent, and Australia, with 17.7 tonnes CO_2 equivalent. For comparison, China's per capita carbon footprint was just 1.8 tonnes CO_2 equivalent. Norway, at 10.3 tonnes CO_2 equivalent per capita, was three times the global average of 3.4 tonnes CO_2 equivalent per capita.

The results for individual countries also reflect the effects of the electricity mix, or the fuel source that countries rely on for electric power. The prevalence of nuclear or hydroelectric power in countries such as Sweden, France, Japan and Norway means that these countries have lower carbon footprints than countries with similar incomes but with more fossil fuels in their energy mix.

For this reason, Ivanova says, a significant portion of household impacts from Sweden and France come from imports (65 and 51 per cent respectively), because the products that are imported are mostly produced with fossil fuels.

An Enormous Database Allows Comparisons

The researchers relied on an extremely large and detailed database that NTNU developed in partnership with colleagues from the Netherlands, Austria, Germany, the Czech Republic and Denmark called EXIOBASE.

The database describes the world economy for 43 countries, five rest-of-the-world regions and 200 product sectors, which allows researchers to ask questions about how different products or countries affect the environment.

They were also able to ask how an average consumer in each of the countries or regions affects the environment as measured by greenhouse gas emissions (tonnes CO_2 equivalent), water use (in cubic metres), land use (in 1000 square metres) and material use (in tonnes).

The 43 countries represent 89 per cent of the global gross domestic product and between 80-90 per cent of the trade flow in Europe, as measured by value.

No Surprises: Take the Bus, Eat Vegetarian or Vegan

The advantage of identifying the effects of individual consumer choices on the different environmental measures is that it pinpoints where consumers in different countries can cut back on their impacts.

"Households have a relatively large degree of control over their consumption, but they often lack accurate and actionable information on how to improve their own environmental performance," the researchers wrote in the journal article reporting their results.

Eventually, the goal is to be able to use this information to guide policy, Ivanova said. The effort is a part of the GLAMURS project, an EU-funded effort designed to promote greener lifestyles and environmentally responsible consumption in Europe.

In the meantime, two easy ways to cut your environmental impact are to stop eating meat, and cut back on your purchases, she said.

Currently, EU consumers spend 13% of their total household budget on manufactured products. If the average EU consumer switches away from spending money on these manufactured products to paying for services instead, this would cut close to 12 per cent of the EU's current household carbon footprint, Ivanova said.

"Any activity where we have a choice of buying a product or using a service, the service will have much less impact," she said.

Urban Residents Can Help Curb Climate Change by Buying Less Stuff

Alejandra Borunda

Alejandra Borunda is a writer with National Geographic and a PhD candidate in Earth and Environmental Sciences at Columbia University.

Cities can play a major role in the global effort to curb climate change, a new report says—and a major step they can take is helping their inhabitants consume a whole lot less stuff by making changes in the way cities are run.

Even the most forward-thinking cities have a long way to go to neutralize their carbon emissions, the report says. That's partly because for years, cities have been doing carbon math wrong, adding up only the carbon costs that occur within city limits. But much of city dwellers' climate impact actually comes from the things they eat, use, or buy that originate far outside the city—from food to clothes to electronics and more.

To keep emissions in check, the report suggests, cities should aim to trim their carbon emissions by 50 percent in the next 11 years, and then by a total of 80 percent by 2050. And because, as the researchers found, a hefty portion of those emissions can be traced back to consumer goods, food, and energy produced outside city limits, one of the best things cities can do is help their residents pull back on consumption.

That's a big challenge but also a big opportunity, says Mark Watts, the lead author of the report and executive director of the C40 city network, an international network of cities committed to addressing climate issues.

"Halving emissions in the next 10 years—that's what needs to happen, and cities see that," he says. "Now, it's time to move onto

"How Can City Dwellers Help with Climate Change? Buy Less Stuff," by Alejandra Borunda, National Geographic Partners, LLC., June 11, 2019. Reprinted by permission.

the next stage, because we're already in a climate emergency, and figure out how does government have to change in order to hit that target?"

The True Cost

Today, some 55 percent of all humans live in urban areas, where they account for about 70 percent of all annual carbon emissions. In the future, demographers predict, even more of Earth's population will likely congregate in cities, hitting about 70 percent by 2050. If nothing changes, carbon emissions from cities is on track to almost double by 2050, the report says. And as cities' carbon emissions go up, so do the planet's.

For years, many cities sold themselves as bastions of efficient, low-carbon living. To some extent, that's true. Densely packed neighborhoods, good public transit systems, and green buildings all help to keep their inhabitants' carbon impacts in check. (Read about what sustainable cities of the future might look like).

But city dwellers—especially those in wealthy cities in developed countries—tend to buy more, fly more, and use a lot more energy than people who live in rural areas. All the things they buy—from the clothes to the food to the electronics and more—have their own complicated and often substantial planetary costs that aren't always immediately obvious.

A t-shirt, for example, might get made of cotton grown in India; be manufactured in China using coal energy to power the sewing machines; packed up in yet another country with oil-based plastic packaging; shipped across oceans in fossil-fuel-fired container ships; and delivered by diesel truck to the store in which they're sold.

A real assessment of someone's carbon footprint takes the carbon footprint of these "consumed" products into account. And when city dwellers' consumption habits are added up, it turns out that urbanites have a carbon toll about 60 percent higher than previous calculations suggested. City dwellers in 96 of the world's biggest cities alone make up a hefty 10 percent of all global carbon emissions each year.

"People tend to forget that most of the products we consume and our personal carbon footprints are imported from elsewhere to give us a great life in the modern cities we live in," says Jeroen van der Heijden, an expert on climate and government at Victoria University in New Zealand.

"If we truly want to make a meaningful contribution to cutting carbon emissions, we must do much better than building green houses. We have to rethink how we live and what we consume."

The Road Ahead Is Paved with Less Stuff

National governments and international communities have struggled to take meaningful steps toward addressing carbon emissions. In many cases, cities have stepped in to fill that role, developing ambitious climate action plans that seek to curb emissions.

The C40 network cities have collectively pledged to limit their carbon emissions to levels that will help keep the planet from warming more than 1.5 degrees Celsius (2.7 degrees Fahrenheit), the upper limit of warming the Intergovernmental Panel on Climate Change recently warned against exceeding.

To get there, the report suggests cities can nudge behaviors in six key areas: food, construction and building, clothing, vehicles and transportation, aviation, and consumer electronics from washing machines to computers to phones.

For example, cities are often already major food purchasers; they buy for schools, city organizations, and more. That means that they can influence emissions by changing their buying practices.

New York schools are starting a "Meatless Mondays" program in 2019 that the city says will reduce its citizens' carbon footprint and make kids healthier. Other cities, like Milan, have put programs in place to help local agriculture thrive, reducing the carbon costs from transporting foods long distances.

It turns out that city dwellers also buy a lot of clothes, and the carbon impact of those jeans and sweaters piles up. If people bought only eight new clothing items each year, the report says, they could cut that impact in half.

Cities can also take action to reduce the amount of energy their denizens use by doing things like tweaking building codes to encourage retrofits of buildings rather than new construction; prioritizing low-carbon transportation options that keep people from buying new cars or motorbikes; and setting up programs that help people extend the lifetime of their electronics and appliances rather than constantly replacing them. Every intervention that helps people buy less new stuff adds up, pushing a city's emissions down.

The transformations have to happen in a way that cuts from the individual consumer all the way up to the big players like the utilities who serve a city, says Patricia Romero-Lankao, an expert on cities and the environment at the National Renewable Energy Laboratory in Colorado.

"Yes indeed we need to change the way we use energy, heat houses, think of our sense of comfort—which is a cultural thing—buy clothes, all that," she says. "But we really also need to work with the utilities, the corporations, the big players whose products we're using."

But the biggest transformation is about a mindset, says Watts, of C40. "We're talking about a really radical change in consumption patterns," he says, moving toward a world where there is much less buying, less building, and less waste. "But the benefits really are huge. Avoiding the climate crisis really does mean building a much better life."

Individual Consumption Choices Drive Societal Change

Steve Westlake

Steve Westlake is a PhD Researcher in Environmental Leadership at Cardiff University in Wales. His research considers the role of pro-environmental behavior and social norms in adopting low-carbon behaviors.

What can we do in the face of the climate emergency? Many say we should drive less, fly less, eat less meat. But others argue that personal actions like this are a pointless drop in the ocean when set against the huge systemic changes that are required to prevent devastating global warming.

It's a debate that has been raging for decades. Clearly, in terms of global greenhouse gas emissions, a single person's contribution is basically irrelevant (much like a single vote in an election). But my research, first in my masters and now as part of my PhD, has found that doing something bold like giving up flying can have a wider knock-on effect by influencing others and shifting what's viewed as "normal."

In a survey I conducted, half of the respondents who knew someone who has given up flying because of climate change said they fly less because of this example. That alone seemed pretty impressive to me. Furthermore, around three quarters said it had changed their attitudes towards flying and climate change in some way. These effects were increased if a high-profile person had given up flying, such as an academic or someone in the public eye. In this case, around two thirds said they fly less because of this person, and only 7% said it has not affected their attitudes.

I wondered if these impressionable people were already behaving like squeaky-clean environmentalists, but the figures suggested not. The survey respondents fly considerably more than average, meaning they have plenty of potential to fly less because of someone else's example.

To explore people's reasoning, I interviewed some of those who had been influenced by a "non-flyer." They explained that the bold and unusual position to give up flying had: conveyed the seriousness of climate change and flying's contribution to it; crystallised the link between values and actions; and even reduced feelings of isolation that flying less was a valid and sensible response to climate change. They said that "commitment" and "expertise" were the most influential qualities of the person who had stopped flying.

Letting Fly

It's not all a bed of roses, of course. Flying represents freedom, fun and progress. It boosts the economy and can provide precious travel opportunities. So suggesting that everyone should fly less, which may seem the implicit message of someone who gives up flying because of climate change, can lead to arguments and confrontation. One person for example said that my gently worded survey was "fascist and misinformed." You don't get that when you ask about washing-up liquid.

My research also probed ideas of inconsistency and hypocrisy. In short, people hate it. If Barack Obama takes a private jet and has a 14-vehicle entourage to get to a climate change conference, or a celebrity weeps for the climate while rocking a huge carbon footprint, it doesn't go down well. And if future laws are introduced to reduce flying because of climate change, it looks essential that politicians will have to visibly reduce their flying habits, too. Other research has shown that calls for emissions reductions from climate scientists are much more credible if they themselves walk the talk.

That people are influenced by others is hardly a shocking result. Psychology researchers have spent decades amassing evidence about the powerful effects of social influence, while cultural evolution theory suggests we may have evolved to follow the example of those in prestigious positions because it helped us survive. Pick up any book on leadership in an airport shopping mall and it will likely trumpet the importance of leading by example.

Which raises the question: if our political and business leaders are serious about climate change, shouldn't they be very visibly reducing their own carbon footprints to set an example to the rest of us? This is now the focus of my research.

But Why Me?

Weaving an invisible thread through all of the above is the thorny issue of fairness and inequality. The wealthiest 10% of the global population are responsible for 50% of emissions, and plenty of that will be due to flying. In the UK, around 15% of people take 70% of the flights, while half of the population don't fly at all in any one year. As emissions from aviation become an ever increasing slice of the total (currently around 9% in the UK, 2% globally) this inequality will become harder for everyone to ignore.

In the mean time, the debate about personal vs. collective action will continue. My research supports the arguments that this is a false dichotomy: individual action is part of the collective. So, while you won't save the world on your own, you might be part of the solution.

Understanding Which Activities Have a Greater Environmental Impact Can Help Reduce Consumption

Morteza Taiebat and Ming Xu

Morteza Taiebat is a joint PhD candidate in Environment and Sustainability as well as Transportation Engineering at the University of Michigan. He is interested in the intersection of transportation energy and environmental sustainability. Ming Xu is an Associate Professor at the School for Environment and Sustainability of the University of Michigan, where his research focuses on sustainable engineering and industrial ecology.

As the public conversation about climate change gets increasingly serious, many Americans may be wondering: How do my individual choices affect climate change?

Household consumption—food, housing, transportation, apparel and other personal services—is an important contributor to greenhouse gas emissions. Everything you eat or wear, or every time you drive, you add to the global total emissions. The typical American's annual per capita carbon footprint is over five times the world per capita average.

A study by our research team, including Kaihui Song, Shen Qu and Sai Liang, published on September 10, sheds light on the global carbon footprint of U.S. households.

1. Some Activities Have a Bigger Impact

We looked at data from 1995 to 2014 from the U.S. Consumer Expenditure Survey, as well as the World Input-Output Database. We looked at the total global warming potential of all greenhouse

"5 Charts Show How Your Household Drives Up Global Greenhouse Gas Emissions," by Morteza Taiebat, Ming Xu, The Conversation Media Group Ltd, September 10, 2019. https://theconversation.com/5-charts-show-how-your-household-drives-up-global-greenhouse-gas-emissions-119968. Licensed under CC BY-ND 4.0.

gas emissions, not just carbon dioxide, as measured in their "carbon dioxide equivalent."

We found that over 20% of all U.S. emissions are directly attributed to household consumption. If you consider indirect emissions, this figure is closer to 80%.

Let's zoom in on the latest available annual numbers, mostly from 2009, which give a better sense of these staggering impacts.

U.S. households generate 5.43 gigatons of carbon dioxide equivalent emissions every year. About 82.3% of those emissions are produced domestically.

The remaining emissions are generated outside the U.S. These emissions come from global supply chains. For instance, the family car might have been manufactured abroad. So emissions from manufacturing of the car are created outside the U.S., but the emissions from tailpipe are domestic.

Transportation and housing contribute over 60% to the total domestic carbon footprint of U.S. households. Supply chain emissions from services—such as health care, banking and lodging—and food contribute the next largest amounts.

Food, furnishing and supplies, and clothing are the three largest drivers of overseas emissions from U.S. households.

2. China Bears the Brunt of Overseas Emissions

The overseas carbon footprint driven by the U.S. households is distributed disproportionately among countries.

The most considerable portion of overseas carbon footprint of U.S. households is actually released in China, followed by Canada, India, Russia and Mexico.

The overseas carbon footprint from Mexico is largely driven by food consumption in the U.S., while fuel consumption in the U.S. was the main driver for overseas carbon footprint from Canada and Russia, where the U.S. gets the majority of its imported oil products and natural gas in that period.

While the most substantial amount of the U.S.'s overseas carbon footprint is from China, it is only 3.0% of China's domestic emissions. The majority of China's emissions comes from the activity of its inhabitants, as well as consumption in other countries beyond the U.S.

On the other hand, Canada, Mexico and Taiwan trace a sizeable proportion of their domestic emissions to U.S. household consumption.

3. Wealthier Families Have a Larger Footprint

A household's carbon footprint generally increases with its income, ranging from 19.3 to 91.5 tons of CO_2-equivalent annually.

The average carbon footprint of the wealthiest households is over five times that of the poorest.

In 2009, households with less than US$30,000 annual disposable income made up 25.7% of the total U.S. population, but were only responsible for 19.3% of U.S. households' carbon footprint.

On the other hand, wealthy consumers with more than $100,000 annual household income accounted for 22.3% of the total population but were responsible for nearly one-third of households' total carbon footprint.

4. The Great Recession Caused a Dip

U.S. households' carbon footprint had been steadily growing from 1995 until 2005, when it began to plateau.

In 2009, the combined domestic and overseas footprint dropped by 8.5% from the previous year, mainly due to the Great Recession.

The share of overseas carbon footprint in total carbon footprint of the U.S. household consumption had been rising steadily and peaked at around 20% in 2006. After 2006, the share of overseas carbon footprint started to decrease, as imports slowed down before the recession.

5. Transportation Makes the Biggest Difference

The variations of household carbon footprint from 1995 to 2014 were largely driven in transportation use, including emissions from vehicle manufacturing, fuel and public transportation.

Transportation emissions, both per capita and per household, have continued to rise over time. This is despite significantly reduced tailpipe emissions from vehicles and nearly 30% improvement in fuel economy of cars in this period. Mandates and standards, such as Corporate Average Fuel Economy (CAFE) at the federal level and Zero-Emission Vehicle (ZEV) at the state level, enabled this rapid progress.

So what's causing the emissions to keep rising? People want to travel more and are more likely to own more household vehicles. Meanwhile, vehicles have a lower average number of occupants. Mass transit and active modes of transportation, like bike riding, are growing slowly.

In 2016, for the first time in history, the emissions from the U.S. transportation sector surpassed the power sector emissions. This fact along with our observation from household carbon footprint from transportation underscore the importance of policy efforts related to emissions from the transportation sector.

Government Must Do More to Address Climate Change

Anders Levermann

Anders Levermann is a climate scientist and a professor at the Potsdam Institute for Climate Impact Research in Germany and Columbia University.

From climate change to child labour, the responsibility for solving major societal problems is increasingly being shifted to the individual. People feel in order to save the world they have to be "good." Yet that is bad—because it paralyses change. Global challenges must be tackled by institutions. That's why the UK's Committee on Climate Change was absolutely right to criticise the government in the strongest terms today for failing to take more action against the climate crisis.

Personal sacrifice alone cannot be the solution to tackling the climate crisis. There's no other area in which the individual is held so responsible for what's going wrong. And it's true: people drive too much, eat too much meat, and fly too often.

But reaching zero emissions requires very fundamental changes. Individual sacrifice alone will not bring us to zero. It can be achieved only by real structural change; by a new industrial revolution.

Looking for solutions to the climate crisis in individual responsibilities and actions risks obstructing this. It suggests that all we have to do is pull ourselves together over the next 30 years and save energy, walk, skip holidays abroad, and simply "do without." But these demands for individual action paralyse people, thereby preventing the large-scale change we so urgently need. We do not just need the 5-10% of the population willing and able to put time, money and effort into change. We need everyone to turn the tide towards sustainability worldwide.

"Individuals Can't Solve the Climate Crisis. Governments Need to Step Up," by Anders Levermann, Guardian News & Media Limited, July 10, 2019. Reprinted by permission.

There is hope that lies in the fact that we do not have to wait for each individual on Earth to become a better person and save the planet. All we need is to create a consensus within society that we should not destroy our home and demand that governments make this their first priority.

Some people argue that this is a cheap and convenient excuse to shift responsibility from the individual to the politicians. But it is neither cheap nor convenient. Each one of us remains individually responsible: to stay informed, to demand something different, and to keep politicians and institutions in check.

We don't expect individuals to take the lead when it comes to other social and economic challenges, such as unemployment. There is a decades-long economic consensus that unemployment should be kept as low as possible. But you would not ask an individual who warned that unemployment was too high: "so, what action do you personally take in the fight against unemployment?" Because that question is absurd. Unless you are the CEO of a big company, or the mayor of a city, as an individual you have no significant impact on unemployment.

The same is true of the climate crisis. What we need is citizens to make adamant demands of their politicians and institutions for more urgent action. Just as no party that pledged to increase rather than reduce unemployment would ever get elected in the UK or any other country, no political party should be allowed to dodge a clear strategy against climate risks. This is a challenge for politics, not for the individual.

In a society where environmentally and socially harmful goods and services are often indistinguishable from environmentally friendly or fair products, it's naive to think that asking the individual to save the world through consumer choice will be effective. And neither is it always the moral thing to do: is it right to demand from an Indian farmer that he cares about climate protection? What about the struggling single mother in London or Berlin with her three children?

If we take civil and human rights seriously, we cannot assign solving global problems to the individual. And the call for greater individual responsibility actually risks becoming detrimental to the cause as it prevents people from realising the scale of political change that needs to happen. Instead of seeing the big picture, people are diverted to the fine print on the refrigerator shelf in the supermarket.

There has been a trend towards shifting responsibility for societal success from our political institutions to the individual. But it's only as a society that we can collectively demand our politicians take the action needed to address the climate crisis.

Corporations Have the Biggest Impact on Climate Change

Joshua Axelrod

Joshua Axelrod is a senior advocate in the Nature Program of the National Resources Defense Council (NRDC). His work focuses on public land protection and conservation, renewable energy siting on public lands, energy transmission, and climate policy. He is based in Washington, DC.

As people around the globe have become increasingly exposed to the impacts of our climate crisis, the entities with perhaps the most power to stop the crisis—corporations—have begun to squirm. Corporations produce just about everything we buy, use, and throw away and play an outsized role in driving global climate change. A recently published report identified that 100 energy companies have been responsible for 71% of all industrial emissions since human-driven climate change was officially recognized. And it's not just the energy sector. According to self-reported numbers, the top 15 U.S. food and beverage companies generate nearly 630 million metric tons of greenhouse gases every year. That makes this group of only 15 companies a bigger emitter than Australia, the world's 15th largest annual source of greenhouse gases.

It's important for us to understand these corporate contributions to climate change, but it's even more important that major corporations drastically reduce their contributions as quickly as possible. Therein lies a serious tension. Many companies have set greenhouse gas reduction targets, but most of those targets fail to include the emissions associated with the entire life cycle of a given corporation's products. This is important because when a company makes a product, that product requires raw materials that created their own emissions during harvest, extraction, refining, etc.

"Corporate Honesty and Climate Change: Time to Own Up and Act," by Joshua Axelrod, Natural Resources Defense Council, February 26, 2019. Reprinted by permission.

(known as upstream emissions); and when a consumer uses that product, there are further emissions that come from the product's use and eventual disposal (known as downstream emissions). Failing to account for or address these emissions means that the vast majority of greenhouse gases attributable to corporations and their products are falling outside of well-publicized corporate climate commitments.

American Tissue Companies: Glossing Over Their Major Emissions

Take Procter and Gamble (P&G) as an example. NRDC and Stand.earth recently published an in-depth look at the impact P&G and a number of its competitors in the tissue sector are having on the world's remaining intact forests. The report found that use of virgin pulp in the production of their toilet paper, facial tissue, and paper towel brands is a major greenhouse gas source. In fact, with annual virgin pulp use at 1.5 million metric tons, P&G's disposable paper, hygiene, and baby care products are estimated to generate 17.8 million metric tons of greenhouse gas emissions each year.[1] That's a big number—equivalent to the annual emissions of 3.8 million passenger vehicles—but P&G's greenhouse gas reduction goal applies to only a tiny percentage of these emissions.[2]

P&G's climate commitment appears to be fairly progressive on paper: reduce annual emissions 50% by 2030. But the devil is in the details. P&G's commitment only applies to what are known in the corporate greenhouse gas accounting world as Scope 1 and Scope 2 emissions. These are emissions generated by a corporation's own facilities—factories, vehicles, power plants—and the emissions generated by third parties from whom the corporation buys energy. These emissions are easy for corporations to measure, and relatively easy for them to control. But they're only a fraction of the true impact of P&G's operations.

What happens if P&G were to include the emissions from the production of its raw materials and the use and disposal of its products (known as Scope 3 emissions in the corporate world) in its emissions reduction goals? Its baseline emissions number grows from 4.3 million metric tons to nearly 215 million metric tons. See the problem? P&G's climate target only applies to 2% of the corporation's estimated emissions and reducing this small sliver by 50% will only lead to an absolute reduction in the corporation's climate footprint of 1%.

And this is only part of the story. P&G, like many other corporations, seems to be omitting substantial volumes of greenhouse gas emissions from its Scope 3 emissions estimates. For example, the company's emissions accounting category of "Purchased goods and services" is where the emissions from harvesting huge volumes of virgin pulp sourced from trees used in its tissue products should appear. P&G's total estimate of its Scope 3 emissions for the climate impact of the extraction and harvest of all the raw materials across all its "purchased goods and services" is nearly 8.6 million metric tons of greenhouse gases. That's a big number, but when we looked at just the lifecycle emissions of the company's virgin pulp use for tissue, hygiene, and baby care products alone, we found that P&G generates 17.8 million metric tons of greenhouse gases annually[1]—a difference from P&G's calculations of 9.2 million metric tons.

How could these two estimates be so divergent? Giving P&G the benefit of the doubt, it is likely that some of the 9.2 million metric ton different is accounted for in the company's production emissions (Scope 1 & 2), and in emissions associated with product use and disposal (Scope 3). Nonetheless, there appears to be a serious shortfall in the company's calculations of Scope 3 emissions—especially since the "Purchased goods and services" segment encompasses whole other supply chains that have their own significant annual emissions (think plastics or the various manufactured chemicals in beauty and cleaning products).

And P&G is not alone, even within the tissue sector. Kimberly-Clark, one of P&G's biggest competitors, appears to underestimate its Scope 3 emissions even more drastically. It uses substantially more virgin pulp in its numerous disposable products—2.4 million metric tons to P&G's 1.5 million. This volume of virgin pulp would be expected to produce 28.5 million metric tons of greenhouse gases annually[3], despite Kimberly-Clark's estimate that all of the company's emissions—Scope 1-3—generate only 17.5 million metric tons of emissions.

What Would Real Environmental Leadership Look Like?

These companies, which purport to be global environmental leaders, have a lot of work to do to address their full climate impacts. Measuring and reporting emissions is a great first step. Ensuring the accuracy of this measurement and transparent reporting would be a good second one. But at the end of the day, any "science-based target," as P&G likes to say, must be a target that applies to all of the emissions a corporation's activities and products are creating—not just those emitted while a product is being made in a factory.

P&G's 50% greenhouse gas reduction target is a worthy goal, but that target should be leading to real world annual reductions of at least 107 million metric tons of greenhouse gases, not 2 million, because of the necessary inclusion of Scope 3 emissions. An essential first step to reducing these monumental, unaccounted for emissions, as NRDC and Stand.earth argue in their new report, would be for P&G to increase the use of recycled pulp in their tissue products. Today, the company uses no recycled content in their household products, even though using recycled pulp emits three times fewer greenhouse gases. Increasing to even 50% recycled content in its tissue, hygiene, and baby care products could lower P&G's annual emissions by 6.2 million metric tons[4], a significant chunk of the reductions the company should make to help the world avoid the worst impacts of climate change.

Government and individual actions are vital to addressing climate change, but corporations, with their outsized influence and power in today's world, have an even larger role to play. They are able to drive policy change, shape consumer preferences, and rapidly respond to the necessities of climate change at a scale and pace beyond any other political or private entity. Meaningful corporate action is not only necessary as climate change accelerates by the day, it is a global obligation. As some of the entities most responsible for putting us in the crisis we're in today, it's time for companies to take full responsibility for their climate footprints.

Endnotes

1. Using Paper Calculator 4.0, this number was derived by inputting 1.5 million metric tons of virgin pulp for use in "Tissue" into the calculator. Calculator results are presented in pounds, which have been converted to metric tons here.

2. P&G doesn't provide exact numbers, but their charts suggest that somewhere around 1.5 million metric tons of greenhouse gases are generated during the productions of its tissue products, which are included in its "Baby, Feminine & Family Care" products segment. This represents 8% of the estimated lifecycle emissions generated by it tissue products.

3. Using Paper Calculator 4.0, this number was derived by inputting 2.4 million metric tons of virgin pulp for use in "Tissue" into the calculator. Calculator results are presented in pounds, which have been converted to metric tons here.

4. Using Paper Calculator 4.0, this number was derived by inputting 1.5 million metric tons of virgin pulp for use in "Tissue" and comparing this to 1.5 million metric tons of 50% recycled pulp into the calculator. Calculator results are presented in pounds, which have been converted to metric tons here.

Just 100 Companies Are to Blame for Over 70 Percent of Greenhouse Gas Emissions

Tess Riley

Tess Riley was a deputy editor on the sustainable business team of the Guardian. She is a journalist whose work focuses on the environment and social justice.

Just 100 companies have been the source of more than 70% of the world's greenhouse gas emissions since 1988, according to a new report.

The Carbon Majors Report "pinpoints how a relatively small set of fossil fuel producers may hold the key to systemic change on carbon emissions," says Pedro Faria, technical director at environmental non-profit CDP, which published the report in collaboration with the Climate Accountability Institute.

Traditionally, large scale greenhouse gas emissions data is collected at a national level but this report focuses on fossil fuel producers. Compiled from a database of publicly available emissions figures, it is intended as the first in a series of publications to highlight the role companies and their investors could play in tackling climate change.

The report found that more than half of global industrial emissions since 1988 – the year the Intergovernmental Panel on Climate Change was established – can be traced to just 25 corporate and state-owned entities. The scale of historical emissions associated with these fossil fuel producers is large enough to have contributed significantly to climate change, according to the report.

ExxonMobil, Shell, BP and Chevron are identified as among the highest emitting investor-owned companies since 1988. If fossil fuels continue to be extracted at the same rate over the next 28 years as they were between 1988 and 2017, says the report, global average

"Just 100 Companies Responsible for 71% of Global Emissions, Study Says," by Tess Riley, Guardian News & Media Limited, July 10, 2017. Reprinted by permission.

temperatures would be on course to rise by 4C by the end of the century. This is likely to have catastrophic consequences including substantial species extinction and global food scarcity risks.

While companies have a huge role to play in driving climate change, says Faria, the barrier is the "absolute tension" between short-term profitability and the urgent need to reduce emissions.

A Carbon Tracker study in 2015 found that fossil fuel companies risked wasting more than $2tn over the coming decade by pursuing coal, oil and gas projects that could be worthless in the face of international action on climate change and advances in renewables—in turn posing substantial threats to investor returns.

CDP says its aims with the carbon majors project are both to improve transparency among fossil fuel producers and to help investors understand the emissions associated with their fossil fuel holdings.

A fifth of global industrial greenhouse gas emissions are backed by public investment, according to the report. "That puts a significant responsibility on those investors to engage with carbon majors and urge them to disclose climate risk," says Faria.

Investors should move out of fossil fuels, says Michael Brune, executive director of US environmental organisation the Sierra Club. "Not only is it morally risky, it's economically risky. The world is moving away from fossil fuels towards clean energy and is doing so at an accelerated pace. Those left holding investments in fossil fuel companies will find their investments becoming more and more risky over time."

There is a "growing wave of companies that are acting in the opposite manner to the companies in this report," says Brune. Nearly 100 companies including Apple, Facebook, Google and Ikea have committed to 100% renewable power under the RE100 initiative. Volvo recently announced that all its cars would be electric or hybrid from 2019.

And oil and gas companies are also embarking on green investments. Shell set up a renewables arm in 2015 with a $1.7bn investment attached and a spokesperson for Chevron says it's "committed to managing its [greenhouse gas] emissions" and is investing in two of the world's largest carbon dioxide injection projects to capture and store carbon. A BP spokesperson says its "determined to be part of the solution" for climate change and is "investing in renewables and low-carbon innovation." And ExxonMobil, which has faced heavy criticism for its environmental record, has been exploring carbon capture and storage.

But for many the sums involved and pace of change are nowhere near enough. A research paper published last year by Paul Stevens, an academic at think tank Chatham House, said international oil companies were no longer fit for purpose and warned these multinationals that they faced a "nasty, brutish and short" end within the next 10 years if they did not completely change their business models.

Investors now have a choice, according to Charlie Kronick, senior programme advisor at Greenpeace UK. "The future of the oil industry has already been written: the choice is will its decline be managed, returning capital to shareholders to be reinvested in the genuine industries of the future, or will they hold on, hoping not be the last one standing when the music stops?"

Top 100 Producers and Their Cumulative Greenhouse Gas Emissions from 1988-2015

COUNT	COMPANY	PERCENTAGE OF GLOBAL INDUSTRIAL GREENHOUSE GAS EMISSIONS
1	China (Coal)	14.32%
2	Saudi Arabian Oil Company (Aramco)	4.50%
3	Gazprom OAO	3.91%
4	National Iranian Oil Co	2.28%
5	ExxonMobil Corp	1.98%
6	Coal India	1.87%
7	Petroleos Mexicanos (Pemex)	1.87%
8	Russia (Coal)	1.86%
9	Royal Dutch Shell PLC	1.67%
10	China National Petroleum Corp (CNPC)	1.56%
11	BP PLC	1.53%
12	Chevron Corp	1.31%
13	Petroleos de Venezuela SA (PDVSA)	1.23%
14	Abu Dhabi National Oil Co	1.20%
15	Poland Coal	1.16%
16	Peabody Energy Corp	1.15%
17	Sonatrach SPA	1.00%
18	Kuwait Petroleum Corp	1.00%
19	Total SA	0.95%
20	BHP Billiton Ltd	0.91%
21	ConocoPhillips	0.91%
22	Petroleo Brasileiro SA (Petrobras)	0.77%
23	Lukoil OAO	0.75%
24	Rio Tinto	0.75%

COUNT	COMPANY	PERCENTAGE OF GLOBAL INDUSTRIAL GREENHOUSE GAS EMISSIONS
25	Nigerian National Petroleum Corp	0.72%
26	Petroliam Nasional Berhad (Petronas)	0.69%
27	Rosneft OAO	0.65%
28	Arch Coal Inc	0.63%
29	Iraq National Oil Co	0.60%
30	Eni SPA	0.59%
31	Anglo American	0.59%
32	Surgutneftegas OAO	0.57%
33	Alpha Natural Resources Inc	0.54%
34	Qatar Petroleum Corp	0.54%
35	PT Pertamina	0.54%
36	Kazakhstan Coal	0.53%
37	Statoil ASA	0.52%
38	National Oil Corporation of Libya	0.50%
39	Consol Energy Inc	0.50%
40	Ukraine Coal	0.49%
41	RWE AG	0.47%
42	Oil & Natural Gas Corp Ltd	0.40%
43	Glencore PLC	0.38%
44	TurkmenGaz	0.36%
45	Sasol Ltd	0.35%
46	Repsol SA	0.33%
47	Anadarko Petroleum Corp	0.33%
48	Egyptian General Petroleum Corp	0.31%
49	Petroleum Development Oman LLC	0.31%
50	Czech Republic Coal	0.30%

COUNT	COMPANY	PERCENTAGE OF GLOBAL INDUSTRIAL GREENHOUSE GAS EMISSIONS
51	China Petrochemical Corp (Sinopec)	0.29%
52	China National Offshore Oil Corp Ltd (CNOOC)	0.28%
53	Ecopetrol SA	0.27%
54	Singareni Collieries Company	0.27%
55	Occidental Petroleum Corp	0.26%
56	Sonangol EP	0.26%
57	Tatneft OAO	0.23%
58	North Korea Coal	0.23%
59	Bumi Resources	0.23%
60	Suncor Energy Inc	0.22%
61	Petoro AS	0.21%
62	Devon Energy Corp	0.20%
63	Natural Resource Partners LP	0.19%
64	Marathon Oil Corp	0.19%
65	Vistra Energy	0.19%
66	Encana Corp	0.18%
67	Canadian Natural Resources Ltd	0.17%
68	Hess Corp	0.16%
69	Exxaro Resources Ltd	0.16%
70	YPF SA	0.15%
71	Apache Corp	0.15%
72	Murray Coal	0.15%
73	Alliance Resource Partners LP	0.15%
74	Syrian Petroleum Co	0.15%
75	Novatek OAO	0.14%

COUNT	COMPANY	PERCENTAGE OF GLOBAL INDUSTRIAL GREENHOUSE GAS EMISSIONS
76	NACCO Industries Inc	0.13%
77	KazMunayGas	0.13%
78	Adaro Energy PT	0.13%
79	Petroleos del Ecuador	0.12%
80	Inpex Corp	0.12%
81	Kiewit Mining Group	0.12%
82	AP Moller (Maersk)	0.11%
83	Banpu Public Co Ltd	0.11%
84	EOG Resources Inc	0.11%
85	Husky Energy Inc	0.11%
86	Kideco Jaya Agung PT	0.10%
87	Bahrain Petroleum Co (BAPCO)	0.10%
88	Westmoreland Coal Co	0.10%
89	Cloud Peak Energy Inc	0.10%
90	Chesapeake Energy Corp	0.10%
91	Drummond Co	0.09%
92	Teck Resources Ltd	0.09%
93	Turkmennebit	0.07%
94	OMV AG	0.06%
95	Noble Energy Inc	0.06%
96	Murphy Oil Corp	0.06%
97	Berau Coal Energy Tbk PT	0.06%
98	Bukit Asam (Persero) Tbk PT	0.05%
99	Indika Energy Tbk PT	0.04%
100	Southwestern Energy Co	0.04%

Blaming Individuals for Climate Change Is Inaccurate but Convenient for Corporations

Morten Fibieger Byskov

Morten Fibieger Byskov is a postdoctoral researcher in international politics at the University of Warwick, where he works with the Interdisciplinary Ethics Research Group and the department of politics. He holds a PhD in practical philosophy from Utrecht University.

W hat can be done to limit global warming to 1.5°C? A quick internet search offers a deluge of advice on how individuals can change their behaviour. Take public transport instead of the car or, for longer journeys, the train rather than fly. Eat less meat and more vegetables, pulses and grains, and don't forget to turn off the light when leaving a room or the water when shampooing. The implication here is that the impetus for addressing climate change is on individual consumers.

But can and should it really be the responsibility of individuals to limit global warming? On the face of it, we all contribute to global warming through the cumulative impact of our actions.

By changing consumption patterns on a large scale we might be able to influence companies to change their production patterns to more sustainable methods. Some experts have argued that everyone (or at least those who can afford it) has a responsibility to limit global warming, even if each individual action is insufficient in itself to make a difference.

Yet there are at least two reasons why making it the duty of individuals to limit global warming is wrong.

Individuals Are Statistically Blameless

Climate change is a planetary-scale threat and, as such, requires planetary-scale reforms that can only be implemented by the world's governments. Individuals can at most be responsible for their own behaviour, but governments have the power to implement legislation that compels industries and individuals to act sustainably.

Although the power of consumers is strong, it pales in comparison to that of international corporations and only governments have the power to keep these interests in check.

Usually, we regard governments as having a duty to protect citizens. So why is it that we allow them to skirt these responsibilities just because it is more convenient to encourage individual action? Asking individuals to bear the burden of global warming shifts the responsibilities from those who are meant to protect to those who are meant to be protected. We need to hold governments to their responsibilities first and foremost.

A recent report found that just 100 companies are responsible for 71% of global emissions since 1988. Incredibly, a mere 25 corporations and state-owned entities were responsible for more than half of global industrial emissions in that same period.

Most of these are coal and oil producing companies and include ExxonMobil, Shell, BP, Chevron, Gazprom, and the Saudi Arabian Oil Company. China leads the pack on the international stage with 14.3% of global greenhouse gas emissions due to its coal production and consumption.

If the fossil fuel industry and high polluting countries are not forced to change, we will be on course to increase global average temperatures by 4°C by the end of the century.

If just a few companies and countries are responsible for so much of global greenhouse gas emissions, then why is our first response to blame individuals for their consumption patterns? It shouldn't be—businesses and governments need to take responsibility for curbing industrial emissions.

Governments and Industries Should Lead

Rather than rely on appeals to individual virtue, what can be done to hold governments and industries accountable?

Governments have the power to enact legislation which could regulate industries to remain within sustainable emission limits and adhere to environmental protection standards. Companies should be compelled to purchase emissions rights – the profits from which can be used to aid climate vulnerable communities.

Governments could also make renewable energy generation, from sources such as solar panels and wind turbines, affordable to all consumers through subsidies. Affordable and low-carbon mass transportation must replace emission-heavy means of travel, such as planes and cars.

More must also be done by rich countries and powerful industries to support and empower poorer countries to mitigate and adapt to climate change.

All of this is not to say that individuals cannot or should not do what they can to change their behaviour where possible. Every little contribution helps, and research shows that limiting meat consumption can be an effective step. The point is that failing to do so should not be considered morally blameworthy.

In particular, individuals living in poorer countries who have contributed almost nothing to climate change deserve the most support and the least guilt. They are neither the primary perpetrators of global warming nor the ones who have the power to enact the structural changes necessary for limiting global warming, which would have to involve holding powerful industries responsible.

While individuals may have a role to play, appealing to individual virtues for addressing climate change is something akin to victim-blaming because it shifts the burden from those who ought to act to those who are most likely to be affected by climate change. A far more just and effective approach would be to hold those who are responsible for climate change accountable for their actions.

Sustainability Will Not Be Possible Until Governments Stop Prioritizing Economic Growth

Federico Demaria

Federico Demaria is an interdisciplinary socio-environmental scientist whose research focuses on the unequal distribution of natural resources and environmental impacts as well as promoting an ecologically sustainable world through degrowth.

Growth for the sake of growth' remains the credo of all governments and international institutions, including the European Commission.

Economic growth is presented as the panacea that can solve any of the world's problems: poverty, inequality, sustainability, you name it. Left-wing and right-wing policies only differ on how to achieve it.

However, there is an uncomfortable scientific truth that has to be faced: economic growth is environmentally unsustainable. Moreover, beyond a certain threshold already surpassed by EU countries, socially it isn't necessary. The central question then becomes: how can we manage an economy without growth?

Enough Is Enough

Kenneth Boulding, the economist, famously said that: "Anyone who believes that exponential growth can go on forever in a finite world is either a madman or an economist".

Ecological economists argue that the economy is physical, while mainstream economists seem to believe it is metaphysical.

Social metabolism is the study of material and energy flows within the economy. On the input side of the economy, key material resources are limited, and many are peaking including

"Why Economic Growth Is Not Compatible with Environmental Sustainability," by Federico Demaria, Resurgence Trust, February 22, 2018. Reprinted by permission.

oil and phosphorus. On the output side, humanity is trespassing planetary boundaries.

Climate change is the evidence of the limited assimilative capacity of ecosystems. It is the planet saying: 'Enough is enough!'.

Mainstream economists—finally convinced by the existence of biophysical limits—have started to argue that economic growth can be decoupled from the consumption of energy and materials.

Trade Off

Historical data series demonstrates that this—up to now—has not happened. At most, there is relative decoupling—a decrease in resource use per unit of GDP. But, there is no absolute decoupling which is what matters for sustainability: an absolute decrease of environmental resources consumption.

The only periods of absolute dematerialisation coincide with economic recession. Trade should also be taken into account, to avoid externalisation of pollution intensive activities outside the EU.

The current economy cannot be circular. The main reason being that energy cannot be recycled, and materials only up to a point. The global economy recycles less than 10 percent of materials; about 50 percent of processed materials are used to provide energy and are thus not available for recycling. It is simple: economic growth is not compatible with environmental sustainability.

The list of nice oxymorons is long—from sustainable development to its reincarnations like green economy or green growth—but wishful thinking does not solve real problems. Increase in GDP leads to increase in material and energy use, and therefore to environmental unsustainability.

No Magic Bullet

Technology and market based solutions are not magic bullets. Faith in technology has become religious: scientific evidence shows that, based on past trends in technological improvement, these are coming way too slowly to avoid irreversible climate change.

For instance, efficiency improvements lead to rebound effects, in the context of economic growth (the more efficient you are, the more you consume; e.g. cars and consumption of gasoline). Renewable energy produces less net energy, because it has a lower EROI (Energy Return on Investement) than fossil fuels. For this, and other reasons, it cannot satisfy current levels of energy consumption, which therefore needs to be reduced.

Most of the world's fossil fuel reserves must be left in the ground, unburned, to keep a global temperature rise to no more than 2°C. In fact, fossil fuels should be called unburnable fuels.

Science sometimes brings bad news. An article recently published in Nature Sustainability argues that: "No country in the world meets the basic needs of its citizens at a globally sustainable level of resource use." The question then is: How can the conditions for a good life for all within planetary boundaries be generated?

The uncomfortable truth to be faced by policy makers is the following: Economic growth is ecologically unsustainable. The total consumption of materials and energy needs to be reduced, starting with developed countries.

De-Growth Strategy

Economic growth might also not be socially desirable. Inequalities are on the rise, poverty has not been eliminated and life satisfaction is stagnant.

Economic growth is fueled by debt, which corresponds to a colonization of the future. This debt cannot be paid, and the financial system is prone to instability.

For instance, scientifically it is not clear how the European Union will achieve a low-carbon economy in the context of economic growth, since it implies a reduction of greenhouse gas emissions to 80% below 1990 levels by 2050.

In fact, climatologists Kevin Anderson and Alice Bows have argued convincingly that: "[F]or a reasonable probability of avoiding the 2°C characterization of dangerous climate change, the wealthier nations need, temporarily, to adopt a de-growth strategy."

Obviously, a transition from a growth society to a degrowth one poses several challenges. However, the emerging field of ecological macroeconomics is starting to address them convincingly.

Happiness Factor

Happiness and economics literature shows that GDP growth is not needed for well-being, because there are other important determinants. High life expectancy is compatible with low carbon emissions, but high incomes are not. Moreover, lack of growth may increase inequalities unless there is redistribution.

In any case, the issue is not whether we shall abandon economic growth. The question is how. Scientific debates around it are on the rise, but I am afraid policy making is behind.

There are good signs: critiques of GDP as an indicator of well-being are common, there are policy proposals and degrowth is entering into the parliaments. This is not new. For example, in 1972 Sicco Mansholt, a Dutch social-democrat who was then EU Commissioner for agriculture, wrote a letter to the President of the EU Commission Franco Maria Malfatti, urging him to seriously take into account limits to growth in EU economic policy.

Mansholt himself became President of the European Commission after only two months, but for too short a term to push a zero growth agenda.

The time is ripe not only for a scientific degrowth research agenda, but also for a political one. As ecological economists Tim Jackson and Peter Victor argued in The New York Times: "Imagining a world without growth is among the most vital and urgent tasks for society to engage in."

CHAPTER 2

Have Companies Effectively Adopted Sustainable Practices?

Overview: Elements of Sustainable Business Development

Fibre2Fashion

Fibre2Fashion is a business-to-business (B2B) portal that is dedicated to offering business solutions and textile-based information to all sectors of the textile, apparel, and fashion industry. It is based in India.

The thought of achieving sustainability was earlier limited to the minds of scientists, social activists and visionaries. Gradually, it entered the corporate domain. At present, it is considered as one of the most important aspects of any progressive and dynamic company. Renowned brands not only give sustainability the highest priority but also see it as a major contributor towards success.

Increasing environmental concerns, stringent rules and regulations combined with public awareness, have changed the outlook of business around the world today. By planning and implementing appropriate strategies and functions like green processes, product developments, energy conservations etc., companies can play an important role in achieving sustainability. Nowadays, companies effectively face the challenge of environmental sustainability.

Companies who do business adopting environmental strategies face three stages. From abiding to the rules of eco-friendly environment and managing environmental risk to developing sustainable and long term strategies. Many companies have changed and many are changing towards more sustainability-oriented business goals.

Green product development is a shining star among other environmental strategies that most companies are adopting. Moreover, reports show that green product development

"Environmental Strategies Adopted by Companies to Achieve Sustainability," Fibre2Fashion, January 2014. Reprinted by permission.

strategy alone cannot contribute towards the target of achieving environmental sustainability. It can only stand up when it is supported by other environmental strategies.

For example, renowned Footwear Company's innovation team has adopted the strategy of avoiding oil-based plastic which resulted into reduced carbon emissions. Dry-dyeing clothes save water, chemicals and energy. Thus, companies are adopting innovations, which are environment friendly and produce better products. There are some strategies discussed below which support the environment as well as the business and have been adopted by companies worldwide.

It is necessary to ensure that all the business aspects such as product life cycle management, operations, Information and technology are effective enough to preserve the environment. The overall strategies of the company to improve business efficiency must include complete environmental obligations and energy consumption guidelines.

Environmental stewardship and energy conservation drive should be followed within the company's supply chain across the globe. Strategies which support cost reduction, increase operating and energy efficiency, lower air, water and soil pollution, save natural resources are the most effective strategies of any company. Companies introduce innovative methods to improve Information and technology operations to enhance the performance, without increasing the energy consumption.

The companies need to respond proactively towards the energy and climate challenges through energy saving strategies. Further, companies are keen to fulfill the public commitments they have made, which are valuable to the society and environment.

However, there should be complete transparency in reporting the progress of these strategies and achievement of the goals.

Number of companies has realized that implementing sustainable business strategies lead to better results and open up new opportunities. The first step of any company towards sustainability is the need to comply with environmental laws. Following national and international environmental regulations improves the company's environmental performance. Some companies not only comply with regulations, but also go a step further by adopting complete sustainable development programmes.

Managing environmental risk is the next step of a company towards achieving sustainability. Industries need to proactively adopt such strategies that will help to solve environmental problems. Companies adopt risk management approach to prevent environmental hazards. This strategy reduces company's expenditure resulting from environmental damage. For example, the air pollutants emitted from textile processes and the wastewaters from these textile operations are hazardous to the environment, if not properly treated.

So, when the textile companies develop strategies, which help them in minimizing air, water and soil pollution during the processes; it indirectly helps them to reduce the expenditure for preventing environmental hazards at a later stage.

In addition, by minimizing waste, preventing pollution and eliminating health and safety risks, the company saves on operating cost too. Some companies organize environmental health and safety (EHS) evaluation, initiate environmental policies and carry out environmental management systems (EMSs). Further, pollution prevention and recycling are some techniques used by companies to transform strategies into achievements.

The final step is implementing the strategies to achieve sustainable development in business. The main goal of implementing the strategies is to create a favorable situation which earns profit along with environmental quality. Today, business strategies include corporate environmental policies, considering the long term economic, environmental and social benefits and needs of their customers.

Sustainable development for a company means adopting strategies and actions, which fulfill the requirements of the company, clients and customers at present; at the same time protecting, upholding and improving the human and natural resources, in value and quality for the future. When the companies are able to preserve natural resources, it supports sustainable development. Companies aim at adopting strategies which can provide clean air, unpolluted water and healthy soil for the future generations.

Benefits of Adopting Strategies for Environmental Sustainability

Companies who have adopted energy efficiency strategies such as changing lights to replacing old computers have resulted in saving up to $1 billion in net operational costs.

Going green not only saves money, but also attracts consumers who care for the environment and thus increases the revenue of the company.

Earlier, companies adopted sustainability strategies so as to comply with the government laws, otherwise they had to pay penalty. Now, leading companies are proactively adhering to the concept of sustainability, as they want to contribute towards environment conservation. Moreover, all central, state and local governments provide incentives to the companies for initiating tasks to conserve environment. It includes exemptions from sales tax, income-tax credit, more depreciation for some capital expenses, cash incentives etc.

Additionally, the company's brand value improves by promoting environmentally responsible activities. This overall results into building a positive image of the company. Also, it attracts employees and helps retain workers in the company.

Industries need to understand that natural resources like water and fuel are limited. When the resources start diminishing, the cost will increase and with passage of time, the industries may not be able to procure the natural resources according to their needs. Therefore, it's the duty of every company to protect these resources and find alternative methods for manufacturing their products and services.

In a survey of around 3000 global executives, nearly two-third of the employees found sustainability necessary to stay in today's competitive market. Renowned apparel and footwear brands are trying to build new business models, products and services by adopting the environmental strategies to achieve sustainability. They believe that innovations made after adopting these strategies will determine future market leaders.

Preserving environment is just one element of the concept 'sustainable development'. Economy and society are the other two important elements. For companies to achieve sustainable development, appropriate strategies need to be planned and implemented in economic, social and environmental areas.

Major Companies Are Adopting Sustainable Practices

Jo Confino

Jo Confino works at the Huffington Post as the executive editor of the "Impact & Innovation" section and the editorial director of the "What's Working" section. He previously served as chairman and editorial director of the Guardian's "Sustainable Business" vertical.

While the vast majority of US companies are asleep at the wheel when it comes to facing up to multiple sustainability challenges, a select group is waking up to the need for urgent action.

In a new report, Ceres, a non-profit focused on sustainable business, lambasted the lack of progress across American corporations in general—but also highlighted some companies that deserve praise.

Critics would rightly say that there is not a single major corporation that is doing enough to adequately confront issues such as climate change and resource scarcity. But Ceres says a small but growing number of companies rank in the "top tiers" of performance across multiple disciplines, ranging from supply chain management to carbon emissions reductions.

Its latest research shows that "companies with strong accountability systems - board oversight, clear policies on human rights and environmental management, active stakeholder engagement and disclosure - in many cases also have strong results on greenhouse gas emissions, use of renewable energy, strong work with suppliers, as well as driving sustainability into product and services".

In order to encourage other businesses to take action, Ceres has shined the spotlight on the following companies:

"Best Practices in Sustainability: Ford, Starbucks and More," by Jo Confino, Guardian News & Media Limited, April 30, 2014. Reprinted by permission.

Board Leadership: Alcoa

A fifth of executive cash compensation is tied to safety, diversity and environmental stewardship, which includes greenhouse gas emission (GHG) reductions and energy efficiency.

Stakeholder Engagement: Pepsico

The food and beverage company presents its sustainability strategy and goals during its annual shareholder meeting and identifies and discloses climate change, water scarcity and public health issues as core sustainability challenges in its annual financial filings.

Employee Engagement: General Electric

GE is using its human resource department to integrate sustainability into the company's culture, ranging from hiring practices and training to employee wellbeing programs.

Water Stewardship: Coca-Cola

The drinks company has improved the efficiency of its water use by 20% and identified the need for a rigorous third-party evaluation of its water management approach.

Supply Chain Management: Ford Motor Company

The car company has established requirements for first-tier suppliers to drive its environmental and social expectations further down the supply chain and works with suppliers to establish GHG emission reduction and energy efficiency targets.

Innovation: Nike

The sports-gear multinational integrates sustainable design across its product portfolio and created the Making app in 2013, allowing the data in its materials sustainability index to be public. This lets designers from across the industry and beyond make more sustainable design decisions, and ultimately, lower-impact products.

Management Accountability: Xylem

The global water technology provider has both a sustainability steering committee and an enterprise risk committee. It identifies senior executives who are held accountable for sustainability performance.

Executive Compensation: Exelon

The energy producer has introduced an innovative long-term performance share scheme that rewards executives for meeting non-financial performance goals, including safety targets, GHG emissions reduction targets and goals engaging stakeholders to help shape the company's public policy positions.

Biodiversity: PG&E

The utility company's environmental policy explicitly references habitat and species protection, and the company publicly reports detailed findings on its efforts.

Investor Dialogue: Starbuck's

At the coffee company's 2013 shareholder meeting, CEO Howard Schultz described the company's efforts to engage with suppliers and local communities where they operate, accelerate investments in sustainable farming and reach Starbucks' goal of ethically sourcing 100% of its coffee beans by 2015.

Disclosure: Brown-Forman

The major distributor of wine and spirits uses ingredients that are both climate sensitive and water intensive. In its 10-K filings with the Securities and Exchange Commission, it demonstrates that it sees sustainability as a way to build consumer relationships and enduring brands. It cites climate change, water scarcity and water quality as significant business risks.

Greenhouse Gas Emission Reductions: Adobe

The software company aims to achieve a 75% reduction, from 2000 levels, in company emissions by 2015. It is using renewable energy technologies, including hydrogen fuel cells and solar arrays, and is also focused on reducing energy needs by improving the cooling efficiency of its data centers and "virtualising" many of its systems, platforms and devices.

Buildings and Facilities: Bank of America

The finance house has committed to increasing its portfolio of Leadership in Energy and Environmental Design (LEED) certified buildings. At the end of 2012, 15% of its total square footage was certified, with plans to increase to a fifth by 2015.

Human Rights: Johnson & Johnson

The pharmaceutical and consumer goods manufacturer has a detailed policy that incorporates the Universal Declaration of Human Rights (UDHR), International Covenant on Civil and Political Rights and International Covenant on Economic, Social and Cultural Rights. It applies these principles not just in its overseas operations and supply chain, but also to all its workplaces.

Sustainable Agriculture: General Mills

The foods company recently released a set of sustainable sourcing commitments that begins with a robust risk assessment process undertaken in partnership with a third party. This approach led the company to prioritise ten commodities, including oats, wheat and corn, that they plan to source sustainably.

Transportation: Walmart

The retail giant is committed to doubling its truck fleet efficiency in the US by 2015. To achieve this goal, it is replacing nearly two-thirds of its fleet with more fuel-efficient trucks, including hybrids.

The company is also collaborating with truck and component manufacturers to build energy-efficient prototype tractors.

Design: Dell

The computer company's integrates alternative, recycled and recyclable materials in its product and packaging design, improvements in energy efficiency, and design for end-of-life and recyclability. One of the company's commitments is to reduce the energy intensity of its product portfolio by 80% by 2020.

Investment in Sustainable Products and Services: Procter And Gamble

The consumer goods multinational reports that it sold $52bn in "sustainable innovation products" between 2007 and 2012, accounting for approximately 11% of the company's total cumulative sales over that period. These are products that provide a greater than 10% reduction from previous or alternative versions in one or more of the following: energy use, water use, transportation, material used in packaging, and use of renewable energy or materials.

Top Companies Are Motivated to Go Green

Rinkesh Kukreja

Rinkesh Kukreja is the owner and author of the blog Conserve Energy Future, which focuses on alternative energy, global warming, recycling, and pollution.

The motivation to go green has not only increasingly become part of many company's corporate social responsibilities but also as an aspect of remaining relevant in the future business environment. Besides, there are more and more environmental concerns that can only be addressed through green initiatives in terms of production, servicing, and manufacturing.

Companies are therefore seeking more innovative methods of promoting eco-friendly environments by integrating green practices in their business functions. The following are the top companies that are taking the lead in incorporating eco-friendly practices by going green.

McDonald's

McDonald's as one of the world's largest food stores are taking the lead in going green by incorporating the outcomes of fast foods on people's health while reducing their overall energy consumption.

Particularly, the company uses energy-efficient appliances thereby cutting energy wastage by 25% during their business activities. McDonald's has also set up green parking lots by preserving them for only hybrid vehicles.

The parking lots equally have permeable concrete with the capability of recharging the vehicles and cleaning groundwater. Furthermore, McDonald's use considerate means to obtain their animal products so as to limit their impacts on destroying animal habitats.

"17 Top Companies That Are Going Green in 2019," by Rinkesh Kukreja, Conserve Energy Future. Reprinted by permission.

Dell

Dell is a leading manufacturer of computer equipment. With the aim of limiting environmental impacts, Dell has promoted the safe disposal of its products by coming up with an effective and efficient recycling program.

Dell allows customers to give back any Dell-branded equipment to the company for free which encourages safe disposal and reduces the overall e-waste count. The company even accepts computers, printers, and monitors from other brands for safe disposal.

Google

Google has also made some tremendous efforts in going green by slashing its energy usage and supporting green energy projects. For instance, Google has constructed the world's most energy-efficient data centers and continuously campaigns for the need for energy conservation and the use of renewable energy sources as well as clean energy products. Google has supported and funded green energy projects by buying and installing numerous windmills and solar panels.

Bank of America

The Bank of America went green when it realized the need for promoting a sustainable environment. Within a period of five years, the bank was able to cut its paper requirements by 32%. The bank also started an internal recycling program and it has achieved success by recycling about 30,000 tons of paper every year.

This translates into conserving about 200,000 trees. What's more, the company offers 3000 dollars cash-back reward to workers who shift to the use of hybrid cars.

Tesla Motors

Telsa Motors is a business involved in the manufacturing of cars that are eco-friendly. The amazing aspect of it is that it does so without forfeiting the power and speed of the cars.

The electric-powered cars made by Tesla Motors are very efficient and can go from 0 to 60 in just 3.9, with a tantamount of 256MPG from its electric output. The cars are sleek and their overall maintenance costs are also cost-effective.

Wal-Mart

Wal-Mart has made significant advances in positioning itself to further green courses in their supply chain operations. As one of the world's biggest retailers, the company startled many and its competitors when it placed a strict policy to cut off suppliers whose manufacturing, processing, and distribution methods contributed to vast carbon emissions.

The Wal-Mart retail stores also utilize 100% renewable energy sources and their transportation systems maintain on fuel-efficiency.

Honda

Honda has taken various steps to be 100% on par with its environmental protection duty as an auto company. The company has invested a lot of resources in producing fuel-efficient vehicles and is constantly seeking ways to develop a hydrogen fuel cell-powered vehicle.

As such, Honda is ranked as one of the most fuel-efficient auto producers in the US. At the same time, the company promises to cut down its carbon dioxide emissions. The company is also carrying out research with the aim of foreseeing a day when most cars will depend on hydrogen fuel as opposed to gasoline.

United (Continental Airlines Before the Merger)

The continental Airline (now United after the merger with united airlines) is another company that joined the worthy course of going green. It spent more than 16 billion US dollars to replace all their airplanes with those that are more fuel-efficient. This aimed at reducing emissions by 5%.

Further, since the year 2000, the airline has managed to reduce nitrogen oxide emissions by 75%. The airline has also employed about a dozen environmentalist staff members who work hand in hand with engine manufacturers to ensure more efficient processes and greener designs. The company also sorts its trash for recycling.

Tesco

Tesco, a British grocery supply chain company, is not left behind in integrating green elements in its processes. Specifically, it offers shoppers who return shopping bags savings.

Besides that, the energy powering its stores is from wind power. It has also heavily invested in recycling, the use of biodiesel trucks for making deliveries, and estimating its carbon footprint on each item sold to have a better approach towards environmental sustainability.

Brooks

Brooks has impressively joined the bandwagon of green-oriented companies introducing a completely biodegradable running shoe. The shoe is as durable as the conventional ones that exist in the market.

The technique used ensures the shoe only begin to biodegrade when it is in an active enclosed landfill. The biodegrading period takes 20 years as opposed to the conventional ones that take about 1,000 years. In other words, this approach can save up to 30 million pounds of landfill dumping within the same 20 year period.

S.C. Johnson

S.C. Johnson, a company dealing with the manufacture of household products, has also joined the league of green companies. Its mission is to lessen the implications its products have on the environment.

On this account, the company has managed to reduce 1.8 million pounds of volatile organic compounds from its Windex artifacts and another 1.4 million pounds of polyvinylidene chloride from Saran Wrap. The company has minimized the use of coal to generate power by replacing most of it with natural gas.

Coca-Cola

Coca-cola has made substantial strides in narrowing down to three most-important environmental goals. These include water preservation, energy and climate protection, and sustainable packaging. These initiatives imply a determination to be environmentally conscious. Accordingly, Coca-cola is actively involved in community recycling programs, the use of efficient energies in production and supplies, and green packaging designs.

Starbucks

Starbucks is known worldwide as a top-ranking coffee shop. Besides that, it's among the list of top companies that are going green. It has managed to do this by enforcing measures such as the bean-to-cup approach and the ingenious use of recycled coffee grounds in the making of their coffee tables.

Starbucks is also in partnership with numerous environmental organizations, one of them being Earthwatch Institute, and continues to execute various environmental initiatives.

Toyota

Toyota, the world's largest car manufacturing company, has also come up with innovative cars that reduce the overall carbon footprint. One of the most outstanding cars is the Prius model which is also celebrated as the world's first mass-market hybrid vehicle.

The car has been sold to more than 38 countries worldwide and even EPA has acknowledged its efficiency in terms of fuel consumption. In the UK, it is categorized as the third least carbon-emitting vehicle.

Pratt & Whitney

Going green takes many aspects. One of them is scaling back on the use of raw materials. This is particularly how Pratt & Whitney company has made it to the list of top companies that are going green.

Pratt & Whitney has cut back 90% of its ingots in the jet engine blades manufacturing process. With the use of this creative method, Pratt & Whitney has managed to lower the number of wasted ingots while at the same time significantly reducing factory emissions.

HP (Hewlett Packard)

Hewlett Packard is another computing company that has consistently undertaken sustainable manufacturing and processes to reduce the harm its products pose on the environment. Particularly, it has taken impressive steps in ensuring the current HP branded materials are 100% recyclable.

It has also revamped its computer disposal strategy by opening various operational e-waste recycling plants across the globe. Further, HP takes back computer equipment of all brands and is committed to the use of renewable energy sources.

Target

Target has realized the positive outcome of keeping an eye on eco-friendly sound business practices. Target has devised an innovative way of going green by introducing an eco-clothing line. The eco-clothing line is fashioned and designed by the environmentally sound and dynamic fabric which limits the over-reliance of raw products.

The retail operations also prioritize on lighting conservation at its shopping centers. Furthermore, Target funds and supports various environmental sustainability programs in the areas of education and environmental conservation.

Sustainability Gives Businesses a Competitive Edge

Knut Haanaes

Knut Haanaes is a Norwegian professor of strategy at the International Institute for Management Development (IMD), which is based in Switzerland. His research focuses on digital practices, corporate strategy, and sustainability.

Sustainability is becoming more important for all companies, across all industries. 62% of executives consider a sustainability strategy necessary to be competitive today, and another 22% think it will be in the future.

Simply put, sustainability is a business approach to creating long-term value by taking into consideration how a given organization operates in the ecological, social and economic environment. Sustainability is built on the assumption that developing such strategies foster company longevity.

As the expectations on corporate responsibility increase, and as transparency becomes more prevalent, companies are recognizing the need to act on sustainability. Professional communications and good intentions are no longer enough.

The following industry leaders illustrate what sustainability initiatives look like:

- Nike and Adidas have both stepped up seriously. Nike has focused on reducing waste and minimizing its footprint, whereas Adidas has created a greener supply chain and targeted specific issues like dyeing and eliminating plastic bags.
- Unilever and Nestlé have both taken on major commitments; Unilever notably on organic palm oil and its overall waste

and resource footprint, and Nestlé in areas such as product life cycle, climate, water efficiency and waste.

- Walmart, IKEA and H&M have moved toward more sustainable retailing, largely by leading collaboration across their supply chains to reduce waste, increase resource productivity and optimize material usage. It also has taken steps to address local labour conditions with suppliers from emerging markets.
- Pepsi and Coca-Cola have both developed ambitious agendas, such as increasing focus on water stewardship and setting targets on water replenishment.
- In biopharma, Biogen and Novo Nordisk have both worked toward energy efficiency, waste reduction, and other ecological measures. They have also focused on social impact via partner initiatives in the areas of health and safety.
- In financial services we see how banks like ANZ and Westpac in Australia both advance local communities with good sustainability practices and by embedding sustainability in their business processes and culture.
- Car manufacturers like BMW and Toyota have made strides on energy efficiency and pollution reduction, not to mention Tesla as an outsider really challenging the industry's overall footprint.

These firms have all made strong commitments to sustainability, in large part through transparency and addressing material issues. They are embarking on a more sustainable journey, and all firms should follow suit over the next decade.

Two Gaps to Beware Of

In order to address sustainability appropriately companies need to bridge two critical gaps:

- "The knowing—doing gap": A study that I participated in by BCG/MIT finds that whereas 90% of executives find sustainability to be important, only 60% of companies incorporate sustainability in their strategy, and merely 25% have sustainability incorporated in their business model.

- "The compliance—competitive advantage gap": More companies are seeing sustainability as an area of competitive advantage, but it is still a minority—only 24%. However, all companies need to be compliant. Management should address these topics separately—not mesh them together. Compliance is holistic, a "must do". For competitive advantage, only a few material issues count.

Companies that stand out in the area of sustainability address both gaps. They have evolved from knowing to doing and from compliance to competitive advantage. They also know the risk of getting this wrong. For instance promising and not delivering, or addressing material issues without being solid on compliance.

Some Practical Recommendations

Just like with overall strategy there is no "one right solution" on sustainability. The best solution depends on the ambitions and stakes at each company. Here are a few useful actions for all management teams to improve sustainability practices.

Align Strategy and Sustainability

Management needs to make sure that the strategy of the company and the sustainability efforts are aligned. Often we see divergence, which of course makes the sustainability efforts fragile, lacking real commitment and prioritization. There are many good examples. Take Unilever's "Sustainable Living" which has the ambition to decouple growth and output as well as reduce its resource footprint by focusing on waste reduction, resource efficiency, sustainability innovation and ecological sourcing (like in organic palm oil). Similarly, Toyota is well known for innovation in hybrid engines, but less so for reducing their dependence of rare earth minerals. These minerals were required for hybrid and electric engines. But by developing alternative motor technologies Toyota reduced its import dependence and operational risk, and in doing so reduced its financial risks in case of price increases.

Compliance First, Then Competitive Advantage

First and foremost companies need to address compliance, which often relates to regulations in waste management, pollution and energy efficiency as well as human rights and labour responsibility. Compliance is also an issue that concerns investors. Recent BCG/MIT data shows that investors increasingly shy away from compliance risks. A full 44% of investors say that they divest from companies with poor sustainability performance.

Reactive to Proactive

Many of today's leading companies in sustainability, like Nike, Coca-Cola, Telenor, IKEA, Siemens and Nestlé have stepped up largely as a consequence of a crisis. For example, Nike faced boycotts and public anger for abusive labor practices in places like Indonesia throughout the 90s, but turned the tide around. In 2005, it became a pioneer in establishing transparency by publishing a complete list of the factories it contracts with and a detailed 108-page report revealing conditions and pay in its factories. It also acknowledged widespread issues, particularly in its south Asian factories. By recognizing the impact of sustainability in a crisis these companies have all developed more proactive sustainability strategies.

Quantify, Including the Business Case

All companies struggle with quantifying the return on their sustainability investments. With regards to compliance this is a straight forward issue. With regards to areas of competitive advantage, however, companies need to link sustainability to a business case. But the ones that actually do form a relatively small group.

Transparency

Transparency is a pre-condition for assessing and improving sustainability practices. You cannot judge without transparency, simple as that. Transparency builds on the idea that an open environment in the company as well as with the community will improve performance. The only way for companies to accomplish transparency is through open communications with all key stakeholders built on high levels of information disclosure, clarity, and accuracy—as well as an openness to recognizing faults and improving practices.

Engage the Board

A full 86% of respondents in a recent survey by MIT/BCG agree that boards should play an active and strong role in sustainability. But, only 42% report that their boards are substantially engaged. Boards are often critical in collaborations with key stakeholders such as NGOs, governments and international Organizations.

Engage your Ecosystem

We see that collaboration is critical for efficient sustainability practices, in particular in solving crises and in shaping broader solutions. The MIT/BCG data shows that 67% of executives see sustainability as an area where collaboration is necessary to succeed.

Finally—and Most Importantly—Engage
the Organization Broadly

One example of engagement is Salesforce.com which through their "1/1/1" philanthropy program contributes to each employees' personal ability to engage with environmental organizations and initiatives that support local communities. Another good example is Nespresso, responding to the debate over the sustainability of its capsules, the company has embedded sustainability into the DNA of every part of its business. Nespresso's very purpose is linked to the so called "Positive Cup" campaign. Sustainability is considered during every decision made at Nespresso. The company seems sincere about reducing its impact and is even looking at its aluminum sourcing.

In sum, sustainability is a major challenge, one that matters beyond individual companies. But reassuringly a number of large companies are developing forward-thinking sustainability policies. It is really becoming clear that sustainability is a megatrend that simply isn't going away!

Companies Are Not Doing Enough to Prevent Climate Change

Alison Moodie

Alison Moodie is a Los Angeles-based multimedia journalist whose work focuses on technology, higher education, and sustainability. She formerly worked as a sustainable business reporter for the Guardian and is currently the health editor at Bulletproof.

Scientists and world leaders have agreed that to avoid environmental catastrophes like super droughts and mass extinctions, the Earth's temperature cannot exceed 2C above pre-industrial levels. But the world is quickly burning through the amount of carbon dioxide it can emit to avoid that level of global warming—and some warn we'll have exhausted the carbon budget within 30 years.

While governments around the world have committed to reducing their emissions, the corporate world is lagging behind, according to a new report from CDP, a London-based nonprofit that collects and distributes data on corporate environmental impacts.

Released Wednesday, the Mind the Science report delivered a sobering set of conclusions about climate change, criticizing companies for failing to adhere to targets that might help avoid catastrophic warming.

The good news is that companies are recognizing the very real threat of climate change and taking steps to mitigate its effects. According to the report, 81% of the world's 500 largest companies have set targets to reduce their carbon footprints.

The bad news is that most companies aren't doing enough. The report looked at 70 of the most energy-intensive companies across the aluminum, cement, chemicals and electric utility sectors. Together, these companies were responsible for 9% of global emissions in 2014.

According to the report, only six of those companies, including Hong Kong-based utility CLP and Swiss cement company Holcim, had set long term targets that were large enough to help keep warming within 2C. Twenty two of the companies haven't publicly declared an emission reduction target, and nine companies don't even monitor or report their CO_2 emissions.

"It's a very significant fraction," said Pedro Faria, author of the report. "It's a point of concern that there is no real transparency in terms of the amount of CO_2 they put into the atmosphere each year."

Of the companies that have set emissions targets, few have long term targets in place that extend beyond 2030. The report suggests that when a company's short term goals expire in the next few years, businesses should set new targets that are more aligned with contemporary climate science.

Faria said setting long term goals—and soon—is especially important for energy-intensive companies, which will likely need to invest in a lot of new, high tech equipment to reduce emissions.

"Their capital assets last decades, so investment made now will have impacts on their emissions in 20, 30 or 40 years," Faria said. "They need to have this long term vision."

But some companies are doing it right. The report highlighted a few that are setting ambitious, scientifically-backed goals.

NRG Energy Inc, the largest US power producer, has committed to cutting its greenhouse gas emissions 90% by 2050, while Italian power company Enel plans to be carbon neutral by then. Swedish retail giant H&M and food group Nestle also have committed to setting long term, science-based targets.

Setting ambitious emissions goals is not only good for the environment, but it's also good for business. According to the report, companies that set CO_2 targets were more profitable than those that didn't, delivering 9.9% in returns over a 12-month period compared to 9.2% for companies without goals.

In conjunction with the report, the CDP on Wednesday announced a global campaign to urge companies to align greenhouse gas emissions targets with climate science. The Science Based Targets Initiative, launched in collaboration with UN Global Compact, the World Resources Institute and the World Wildlife Foundation, aims to enlist 100 companies by the end of this year and 250 companies by 2020.

"These companies know that science-based targets are in their long term interest, and they are ready to lead in the low carbon economy of the future," said Cynthia Cummis, deputy director of the Greenhouse Gas Protocal at the World Resources Institute, a global research organization that focuses on sustainability. "We hope this critical mass will be the tipping point to making science-based emissions targets standard business practice."

Companies Are More Focused on Short-Term Profitability than Long-Term Environmental Impacts

Andrew Winston

Andrew Winston is the author of numerous titles on climate change and sustainability, including Big Pivot and Green to Gold. He works to inspire companies to help solve climate change.

A re managers particularly concerned about the impacts of climate change on their businesses? If we believe the results of a recent MIT Sloan and BCG survey, the answer is no. But it may not be that dire.

First the sobering survey results: Only 27% of respondents agreed strongly that climate change is a risk to their business—which is frightening when you think about what that says about companies' level of readiness for the significant changes that are upon us already (extreme weather, disruptions to operations and supply chains, and the changing expectations of customers and employees). Additionally, only 11% ranked climate change as a very significant issue.

In a good overview of these survey results published in the MIT Sloan Management Review, editor Nina Kruschwitz voices a legitimate concern that their findings don't jibe with other reports lately, in particular an article in The New York Times titled, "Industry Awakens to the Threat of Climate Change." That story focuses on how the World Economic Forum, and some specific companies like Coca-Cola and Nike, are taking the issue seriously.

Although the two stories seem at odds, they may be describing versions of the same reality. Part of the disconnect stems from what's said by company leaders versus what a broad selection of managers think. A growing number of companies are publicly

"How Much Do Companies Really Worry About Climate Change?" by Andrew Winston, Harvard Business School Publishing, March 4, 2014. Reprinted by permission.

declaring support for strong climate policy—Apple just signed onto the Climate Declaration, joining Nike and many others. But within the ranks of these leading companies, I'm sure there are wide-ranging views, from supportive to skeptical or even hostile.

But the bigger gap is likely a perception of what "climate change" means to survey respondents. Many may think of the issue narrowly as rising temperatures, or as something their companies should manage only for philanthropic, good-for-the-planet reasons.

What Nike and Coca-Cola leadership get is that the climate issue is a systemic problem, not easily defined in one single way, and it directly and profoundly affects their business. Water availability, for example, is in the process of shifting, sometimes dramatically, which means more water and rains in some areas, and much less in others. Extreme weather brings unpredictable dangers for physical assets or massive disruptions to supply chains (like auto and hard drive companies found out with floods in Thailand in 2011).

Most survey respondents probably miss these systemic issues. And very few would consider the much softer elements of risk and value around climate change—like whether employees and customers believe the company is doing enough on the issue.

Nonetheless, companies' understanding of climate change is in fact shifting subtly as more understand the problem as one of risk to be managed—not a scientific or political debate about absolute certainty, but a conversation about possible futures. When risk officers and smart business leaders look at climate this way, they can have productive conversations about how to build more resilient enterprises.

So the real issue of concern that the survey uncovers is not a lack of belief in climate change per se, but a gap in readiness for volatility: Only 9% of respondents thought their organizations were really prepared.

On the one hand, there may not be too much to worry about in this finding. The same perception gap about defining climate change may make managers blind to how much their companies are already doing to reduce carbon and energy use, and thus reduce one element of risk—reliance on volatilely priced fuels. A fleet efficiency project, which many would just call good business with a good payback, is a carbon and climate action. So are a lighting retrofit, a boiler overhaul, innovation to reduce energy use of your products, and much more.

That said, the respondents might be right in the larger sense that companies are unprepared for systemic and longer-term challenges. In my experience, most companies are risk-averse and like to fashion themselves as great "fast followers." But Kruschwitz makes an important point: "Being a fast follower on climate change…may be more complex and require longer lead times than most companies are anticipating." That's exactly right. You can't re-arrange supply chains to avoid droughts or storm risk quickly, or flood-protect or move your facilities on the fly.

Companies are in general bad at thinking long-term and preparing for multiple contingencies (it goes against being lean and maximizing short-term earnings). I believe we need fundamentally new modes of operating that create more resilient enterprises, or what I'm calling "the big pivot" in my forthcoming book.

Companies will, among other things, need to fight the short-termism that plagues business, set goals based on science to drastically cut carbon fast enough, innovate in heretical new ways, and collaborate with friends and enemies alike.

So does it matter much if your company's managers think about "climate change" as a problem in and of itself? In a sense, no, since there is so much a company can do without everyone agreeing on that issue. But the companies that do get it will be able to set their sights and goals differently, and rally passionate employees to really change how they operate. Those more engaged organizations will be more innovative and have a leg up in a hotter, scarcer world.

New Corporate Leadership Is Necessary for Businesses to Go Green

David Broadstock

David Broadstock is an assistant professor of economics in the School of Accounting and Finance at the Hong Kong Polytechnic University, where he also serves as Deputy Director of the Centre for Economic Sustainability and Entrepreneurial Finance.

S ustainability is the backbone of business—this has always been true and for largely obvious reasons. Any organisation which is absent of sustainability is destined to, at some point or another, fail. Typically this is not a desirable outcome for an organisation. So sustainability is the name of the game.

In today's society what exactly do we have in mind when referring to sustainability? I will elaborate on the concept under two broad themes: economic, and environmental.

"Economic sustainability" can be taken as meaning a combination of (i) remaining commercially viable (both now and ideally across future generations) and (ii) being able to sustain operations in the face of unexpected and severe events, such as the global financial crisis which struck in 2007/8 for example.

Economic sustainability can be viewed through five capitals, which include:

- Natural capital which comes from our ecological system;
- Produced capital which comes from our productive activities;
- Human capital which comes from our talented people;
- Social capital which comes from social trust and social interaction; and
- Financial capital which connects all the previous four capitals to help grow and sustain an economy.

"Environmental sustainability" is more directly focused on the physical environment. Insofar as I wish to give it a precise definition, in the organisational context it loosely refers to taking responsibility for the environmental impacts connected—either directly or indirectly—to operational activities.

Economic and environmental sustainability are closely linked in several ways, and will become increasingly more so. Producing goods and services requires, to a greater or lesser degree, the use of natural resources—and thus comes attached with an environmental cost.

Additionally, pollution results from the discharge of (possibly transformed or processed) production inputs into the natural environment, and thus represents waste and inefficiency.

Is it possible that organisations can benefit, i.e. create economic gains, from being focused on environmental sustainability? Evidence of the commercial value attached to environmental sustainability suggests the answer to be yes, as can be gauged by looking at the empirical practise of corporate social responsibility (CSR) reporting.

In brief, CSR reporting offers a (often voluntarily adopted) mechanism for organisations to give customers, clients and other interested parties a detailed overview of the environmental impacts connected to their operations. CSR reporting has become widely practised in industry—a point recognised within a previous South China Morning Post article "Taking a three-pronged approach to achieving business sustainability," by Carlos Lo and Eric Ngai.

So how do the commercial gains arise? Do stakeholders and investors "reward" an environmental conscience? It would be nice to think so, and in some rare cases this may in fact be so, but it is easier to justify corporate "environmental-altruism" by appealing to the commercial opportunities that can be created. [Altruism defined as the process of sacrificing personal gains for the good of the greater society].

Environmental accounting is the business process which underpins the commercial value-added, offering management of financial capital in conjunction with natural capital. Practising environmental accounting helps to identify inefficiencies due to excessive waste discharge and poor use of inputs within the value chain.

Minimising these inefficiencies through careful waste management translates directly into reduced costs, and does not require lowering output. As such, environmental accounting serves to increase the profit margin when applied effectively.

However, across the majority of organisations the function of monitoring, regulating and managing environmental issues has historically been considered out-of-scope. There is a general knowledge gap among society, from which follows a general training gap in organisations.

Organisations require a new training regime that can offer a modern generation of entrepreneurs and leaders the right set of tools to balance both economic and environmental sustainability. Accountants also need to be burnished with new skills in valuing—to an auditable standard and quality—environmental impacts/costs consistently, such that firms could benefit from the potential efficiency gains from environmental accounting.

A common theme connecting economic and environmental sustainability is that managers must take a long term perspective and consider multiple stakeholders in managing each. A consistent pattern among commercial projects is that environmentally friendly projects tend to offer lower returns then "less friendly" ones.

Looking towards the future, it is then fair to posit that entrepreneurial finance will be important in sustaining natural capital. Crowd funding, venture capital, private equity, Green bonds and internet finance are among a range of modern financial instruments that could play a defining role in supporting environmentally sustainable investments and supporting economic sustainability within organisations.

CHAPTER 3

Should Consumption and Production Be Regulated?

Overview: International Efforts to Support Sustainable Consumption and Production

United Nations Environment Programme

The United Nations Environment Programme (UNEP) sets the environmental agenda and promotes implementation of sustainable development within the UN system. It advocates for global environmentalism.

Sustainable Consumption and Production (known as SCP) is about doing more and better with less. It is also about decoupling economic growth from environmental degradation, increasing resource efficiency and promoting sustainable lifestyles.

We are currently consuming more resources than ever, exceeding the planet's capacity for generation. In the meantime, waste and pollution grows, and the gap between rich and poor is widening. Health, education, equity and empowerment are all adversely affected.

Crucially, SCP can contribute substantially to poverty alleviation and the transition towards low-carbon and green economies. To do this, SCP requires building cooperation among many different stakeholders as well as across sectors in all countries.

Sustainable consumption and production refers to "the use of services and related products, which respond to basic needs and bring a better quality of life while minimizing the use of natural resources and toxic materials as well as the emissions of waste and pollutants over the life cycle of the service or product so as not to jeopardize the needs of future generations".

SCP is a holistic approach and is about systemic change. It is built around three main objectives:

- Decoupling environmental degradation from economic growth. This is about doing more and better with less,

"Sustainable Consumption and Production Policies," United Nations Environment Programme. Reprinted by permission.

increasing net welfare gains from economic activities by reducing resource use, degradation and pollution along the whole life cycle, while increasing quality of life. 'More' is delivered in terms of goods and services, with 'less' impact in terms of resource use, environmental degradation, waste and pollution.

- Applying life cycle thinking. This is about increasing the sustainable management of resources and achieving resource efficiency along both production and consumption phases of the lifecycle, including resource extraction, the production of intermediate inputs, distribution, marketing, use, waste disposal and re-use of products and services.

- Sizing opportunities for developing countries and "leapfrogging". SCP contributes to poverty eradication and to the achievement of the UN Millennium Development Goals (MDGs). For developing countries, SCP offers opportunities such as the creation of new markets, green and decent jobs as well as more efficient, welfare-generating natural resource management. It is an opportunity to "leapfrog" to more resource efficient, environmentally sound and competitive technologies, bypassing the inefficient, polluting, and ultimately costly phases of development followed by most developed countries.

Want to know more? Visit the SCP Clearinghouse, a unique one-stop hub dedicated to knowledge sharing, cooperation and innovation for SCP implementation around the world. It brings together the actors of the SCP community at all levels – governments, civil society, the business sector and other stakeholders.

Sustainable Procurement

Public spending, which accounts for an average of 12% of GDP in OECD countries, and up to 30% in developing countries, wields enormous purchasing power. Shifting that spending towards more sustainable goods and services can help drive markets in the direction of innovation and sustainability, thereby enabling the transition to a green economy.

What is SPP?

Sustainable public procurement (SPP) is a "process whereby public organizations meet their needs for goods, services, works and utilities in a way that achieves value for money on a whole life-cycle basis in terms of generating benefits not only to the organization, but also to society and the economy, whilst significantly reducing negative impacts on the environment."

Through SPP, governments can lead by example and deliver key policy objectives and send strong market signals. Sustainable procurement allows governments to reduce greenhouse gas emissions, improve resource efficiency and support recycling. Positive social results include poverty reduction, improved equity and respect for core labour standards. From an economic perspective, SPP can generate income, reduce costs, support the transfer of skills and technology and promote innovation by domestic producers.

How Is UN Environment Active in SPP?

UN Environment has recently coordinated two major projects in sustainable public procurement. The first is Eap Green, which ran from 2013-2016 and involved Ukraine, the Republic of Moldova and Belarus. Second, the SPP and Eco-labelling Project (SPPEL) ran from 2013-2017 with activities in Vietnam, Brazil, Mongolia, Morocco, Costa Rica, Ecuador, Colombia, Peru, Argentina and Chile.

Making the Switch to More Sustainable Consumption and Production Patterns

With funding and support from the European Commission, UN Environment has coordinated the SWITCH initiatives in three regions, aimed at making consumption and production patterns more sustainable.

SwitchMed, Switch-Asia and SWITCH Africa Green have provided support to communities, entrepreneurs and businesses in Mediterranean countries, Asia and Africa respectively, providing tools and connections for social and eco innovations. Visit the websites to find out more!

The Government Is Responsible for Ecological Conservation

Food and Agriculture Organization of the United Nations

The Food and Agriculture Organization of the United Nations (FAO) is an agency of the UN that leads international efforts to achieve food security, defeat hunger, and ensure access to high-quality food for people around the world.

A clear responsibility for conserving a country's basic resources rests with governments. Whether it is the national government that provides the principal leadership, as in the USA, or provincial governments, as in Australia, government at some level must take the initiative for establishing a conservation programme.

While the plan of action for each country will be different, a typical programme will include provisions for a conservation agency, research, an extension service and technical training. It should also provide for incentives and new institutions to encourage farmers to adopt conservation practices. Governments will have to assume that portion of the costs of soil conservation that benefit society as a whole, rather than individual farmers.

Securing popular support for a soil conservation programme is no easy matter. Soil conservation tends to be given low priority, even in programmes to improve agriculture, because immediate economic returns are not apparent. It will be necessary to convince rural and urban leaders that soil erosion leads to lower crop yields and higher food prices, while steadily eroding a country's self-sufficiency.

Advocates of resource management will have to make it clear that the cost to the country of soil degradation may be very great and measurable in terms of more food imports, malnutrition,

"Government's Responsibility for Conservation," Food and Agriculture Organization of the United Nations.

and even starvation. The arguments must be persuasive, because government spending for conservation will have to be substantial during the next two decades if soil degradation is going to be arrested. FAO studies estimate that needed investments in soil and water conservation in 90 developing countries should total $1.5 billion in the year 2000. While the figure may seem high, it is only a tenth of the investment proposed that year for irrigation and one-twentieth of that proposed for mechanization. Further, much soil conservation work is not necessarily capital-intensive and much of the labour can be done by farmers themselves.

Base Policy on Resource Assessment

A country's soil conservation programme should be based on a thorough assessment of its natural resources, including their current condition and the cost of repairing any damage already done to them. Ways to obtain such information will be discussed in Chapter 6. When the resource assessment is complete, a government should establish a national land use or resource policy to guide the development of a conservation programme, as well as other activities for the improvement of agriculture.

Policies will vary widely between countries, depending on their needs and goals. In one country, it might emphasize watershed development, forest management, and the need for local forest product industries. In another, it might call for an improvement in grazing lands—for more cattle and fewer goats—and possibly for relocation of some people in overcrowded areas. In still another country, the chief policy goals might be to improve crop yields 50 percent and to bring additional land into production. In all countries, it might well be a goal to increase farm income and bring about a general improvement in living standards of rural people.

Single Agency Preferred

After a country adopts a land use policy, it will be ready to develop and fund an agency to carry out its conservation activities. There are cogent arguments for establishing a single soil conservation agency in the government, rather than distributing the functions among several ministries or departments. A single agency can do a more effective job of promoting soil conservation because that is its central, rather than peripheral, task. There is the obvious reason of avoiding confusion and duplication of effort. Also, the head of a conservation agency can represent the conservation interest in the process of budgeting of money and manpower. Without such a single-minded advocate, it is unlikely that conservation will receive the continuing support from government that it requires.

One reason why so few countries have single resource agencies and comprehensive conservation laws is because, over the years, separate pieces of resource legislation have been passed one at a time, as each need was recognized. More single-purpose resource laws are concerned with forestry than with any other subject. In countries that have forests, the existence of laws for their protection and management is nearly universal. A smaller number of countries also have soil conservation laws, while countries of the Near East and North Africa have given more attention to grazing laws.

Only a few countries have comprehensive laws covering management of all natural resources. New Zealand, for example, has separate laws covering mining, forests, all phases of animal production, and various other types of agriculture, but it also has a single watershed and soil conservation law broad enough to cover all land use. In Zambia, a comprehensive resources law applies to the conservation of all natural resources, and the minister of land and natural resources has broad authority to define what comes under the law.

But these countries are exceptions.

Drafting Nationwide Laws Difficult

Variations in climate and topography and in local needs and conditions have made it difficult for many governments to draft resource management laws that are equally fair or effective in all parts of their countries. In some places, a minister or a local authority is delegated the power to frame compulsory land use rules as the need arises. This delegation permits more flexible regulation that meets local requirements.

Resource legislation that is too coercive or that is poorly understood may, for one reason or another, go unenforced. Sometimes the emphasis on programmes changes when political leadership is changed. For example, before independence Kenya had a limited soil conservation programme. Under land use rules made under the Agricultural Act, charges were brought against people who failed to build and maintain terraces on steep land. Enforcement of the law was relaxed after Kenya became independent. As a result, most terraces were neglected or ploughed and erosion increased. Today the government recognizes the seriousness of land degradation and has adopted new programmes of corrective action.

One Kenya law, for instance, makes it an offence to clear or cultivate land if its slope is above a certain gradient. A chance to enforce this regulation came when farmers sought to register their land holdings with the new government. No registration was granted for steep land unless terraces were first installed to prevent soil loss.

Legislative solutions are also possible for problems created by tenancy. A law can be passed that allocates the cost and profit from soil and water conservation measures between tenant and landlord. In Uruguay, conservation works constructed by a tenant must be paid for by the landlord at their value when the tenancy is ended. On the other hand, a tenant who refuses to follow official conservation practices may be evicted.

Punitive Laws Are Ineffective

In the USA, one of the 50 States has passed a law imposing penalties on farmers who allow too much soil to erode from their land. In a recent survey of American farmers, however, a large majority opposed any coercive measures on a national level, preferring the present voluntary programme to a mandatory one.

Generally speaking, regulatory approaches to soil conservation are as ineffective as they are unpopular. It is the local farmer who must apply the conservation measures called for, and he must have the knowledge, equipment, capital, and desire to apply them. Incentives and technical assistance are far more successful approaches to getting conservation on the land than punitive action.

Innovations in farming that are too radical may also run into resistance. Most people want to improve what they already have, not change to another system. Any proposal that tears down an existing culture defeats the purpose of a conservation assistance programme. Successful technical assistance requires a broad understanding of the rural people being served their values, their fears, and their goals. Even so, it often takes a long time to persuade land users to adopt improved systems of agriculture.

But it can be done. Japan is an example of a country that has successfully altered its institutions to permit a more productive agriculture. After the Second World War, Japan strengthened its farm-supply and marketing industries, established farm organizations and more agricultural colleges, and developed an extension system. An already existing tradition of conservation was encouraged and supported. These changes, combined with improved crop varieties and more fertilizer and other inputs, helped push rice production in Japan from a prewar average of four tons per hectare to about eight tons per hectare some four decades later. And resources are being managed for sustained use.

Improvement "Packages" Must Attract Farmers

An important key to this kind of success is for the government to have a good "package" of improvements to present to the farmer. The package should offer, not only improved resource protection, but also the promise of greater crop yields for about the same expenditure of labour. If possible, it should mean higher farm income.

In many parts of the world, it is common for a farmer to agree with an extension worker that a certain conservation practice is needed and useful. He will even resolve to adopt it the following season, and then do nothing about it, year after year. The reason for his failure to act is because of economic factors; he is not convinced that adopting the practice will pay.

On the other hand, for example, a drastically different system of wheat farming, promoted by soil conservationists in Western Australia, became an accepted practice among farmers within a relatively short time. It did so because it made economic sense from the start and picked up the enthusiastic support, not only of farmers, but of economists, bankers, and farmer organizations. This experience suggests that researchers who have not yet developed improved systems of farming that also result in more farm income had better keep searching. What is needed is not the best technical solution to resource problems, but the best solution that is acceptable to farmers.

Assuming the country has a system worth promoting, it is essential to train and equip a competent extension service to carry the concept into rural areas. In the USA, the number of technical people in the field to assist farmers solely with soil and water conservation totals about 10 000. If a conservation agency lacks its own extension people to work directly with farmers or villagers, it will have to train and use general agricultural extension workers. If it does, it will have to keep reminding extension people that their job is not only to increase production, but also to make sure than the soil is maintained to grow the crops of the next generation.

Unfortunately, only a handful of developing countries have a cadre of dedicated agricultural extension workers today, much less a service that is adequately staffed and trained. Problems of recruiting are numerous. Some of the more serious constraints to improving extension services in developing countries include:

- lack of interest in agriculture by many students with formal education. To many, farming is the occupation they went to school to escape;
- lack of experience in agriculture by students with town and city back grounds;

- reluctance by college-trained professionals to do the field work necessary to transfer textbook knowledge to practical applications;
- lack of prestige for agricultural positions compared with positions in administration, commerce and industry, foreign affairs, or the military;
- inadequate preparation of students in mathematics and elementary sciences, so that they require additional training to prepare them for conservation courses.

These constraints reflect the generally low esteem in which agriculture is held by many government officials and national leaders. These attitudes must be turned around through conscious national policies before a competent extension service can be enlisted and trained.

Conservation Teams Include Many Disciplines

The most useful technical assistance to rural people is provided by multidisciplinary teams. Conservation teams should include professionals trained in several disciplines—agronomy, civil and mechanical engineering, soil science, hydrology, economics, and rural sociology. Each professional should also receive rudimentary training in disciplines other than his own to gain appreciation of contributions of others to the overall task.

An engineer should know enough economics to realize that the structures he plans and builds must return enough benefits to the community to pay for their cost. An agronomist should know enough sociology to understand that a farmer may reject a perfectly good farming system for reasons which have nothing to do with its agricultural merits. Mutual understanding among team members is requisite to a successful multidisciplinary approach.

A well trained extension worker can also make sure that each new practice accepted by farmers forms part of a larger plan for the general improvement of agriculture. Most farmers adopt new practices in a piecemeal fashion; they usually try out those recommendations that hold promise of increased income. But an extension worker with multidisciplinary training keeps the ultimate objective in mind—to achieve higher farm production on a sustainable basis. He understands how resource management fits in the total farming system, just as he understands the importance of other inputs, like good seed, fertilizers, and control of plant diseases and pests.

This places a heavy responsibility for the success of any programme on the extension worker, but is a responsibility that cannot be fulfilled at any other level. At the national or provincial level, the soil conservation agency should concentrate on applied research, on training extension people, and on supporting their efforts with guidebooks, posters, and other training aids. National leaders cannot generally work face-to-face with the farmer but the field worker can do that.

Local Officials Ensure Success

Local government officials also have a role in carrying out a successful conservation programme. Officials of local governments are better informed on local needs and conditions than central government officials. If possible, local officials should be a link between national policy and farmer action.

In the USA, which has had a Soil Conservation Service (SCS) since 1935, this essential link is provided by 2700 local soil conservation districts. The affairs of each district are directed by a board of from five to seven local people, typically farmers and ranchers, who are elected to office by other farmers or by the general public. Usually they serve without pay.

These local officials are responsible for setting soil conservation priorities in their districts and for carrying out information campaigns. Occasionally, they rent machinery to farmers, sell trees at cost for windbreaks, or testify on conservation needs before county or state committees. Technical assistance to individual farmers from SCS field workers is provided only with the approval of these local boards.

Many believe that the existence of conservation districts is the chief reason why the US Soil Conservation Service has survived for so long. Certainly the arrangement has been popular with land users, who are much more likely to accept guidance from friends and neighbours than from government employees from outside the community. They also feel free to describe experience and express opinions to district board members, who in turn can relay this information to the national conservation agency, where policies may be changed or modified.

Landusers Form Associations

In many countries, successful group action in conservation is achieved through cooperative associations of landowners, tenants, and farmers. An extension of this idea to countries without organized associations should help bridge the gap of understanding between government policy makers and farmers and lead ultimately to better conservation and land use.

Wherever barriers exist to the adoption of conservation measures, it is the responsibility of government—at all levels—to identify those barriers and to attempt to surmount them. Improved institutions may be the answer. Liberal agricultural credit, better seed and fertilizer, and equipment hire and purchase assistance can either improve soil directly or make it possible for farmers to adopt needed conservation measures. Lack of proper machinery, for example, can be an absolute bar to certain soil conservation activities. On the other hand, the development of a new tool or a disease-resistant variety of crop can make a new system of conservation farming profitable for the first time. In agriculture, a single factor in a farming system can have impact on many other factors.

Incentives Are Necessary

Most developed countries have found some form of incentive useful or even essential in encouraging farmers to practice soil conservation. Financial help may come in the form of direct payments to farmers, preferential credit, or low-cost or free use of equipment.

Direct payments seem to produce results, but they require supervision to make sure they are used for the purposes intended. In the USA, a limited amount of government cost-sharing is available to farmers to finance the cost of conservation measures, like terraces and drains. The amount of the cost-sharing and the specific practices covered are determined at the local level. Recently, several states have adopted their own cost-share programmes.

In New Zealand, the Soil Conservation and River Control Council has broad powers to make grants or loans under a variety of conditions. In Nigeria, costs of building terraces by hand were shared on a project between farmers and the government. Each farmer contributed one day of labour each week as his share, while he was paid wages by the government for the other five days. Acceptance of this approach was reportedly much better than on projects where the government carried out the work without involving the farmers.

Another approach to getting more conservation on the land is through tax incentives that allow a farmer tax credit for investments made in conservation practices .

Direct Payments Have Drawbacks

A common problem with direct incentive payments is that the recipients often regard them as a deserved reward for good soil management and stop using conservation practices if the payments are interrupted. This dependent attitude on the part of farmers is largely avoided with preferential loans, which can be made for conservation purposes with low interest and generous terms for repayment. One means of ensuring a conservation loan would be to allow liability for repayment to depend on yields. This would remove the risk of impossible debt, which haunts many small farmers. Loan officials can also encourage more conservation. Many private bankers in the USA will make loans on farms only if the land is under a conservation plan.

Attitude to Short-Term Conservation Costs

If conservation systems always put money into a farmer's pocket, it would be unnecessary for governments to offer so many incentives or to assume so much of the total investment. For the farmer, however, short-term conservation costs often exceed anticipated benefits. Three agricultural scientists in the US Corn Belt tried to find out if building terraces on sloping lands could be economically justified from the farmer's standpoint. They concluded that, except in a few cases, the farmer will sacrifice income to control erosion. Other studies have produced similar results.

But the same conservation measures that are not perceived as economic to farmers may be highly economic to the country as a whole. Ensuring the continuity of the resources necessary for agriculture should be the deciding factor for investments in soil conservation.

Enforcement of International Environmental Protection Laws Must Be Improved

United Nations Environment Programme

The United Nations Environment Programme (UNEP) sets the environmental agenda and promotes implementation of sustainable development within the UN system. It advocates for global environmentalism.

The first-ever global assessment of environmental rule of law finds weak enforcement to be a global trend that is exacerbating environmental threats, despite prolific growth in environmental laws and agencies worldwide over the last four decades.

Despite a 38-fold increase in environmental laws put in place since 1972, failure to fully implement and enforce these laws is one of the greatest challenges to mitigating climate change, reducing pollution and preventing widespread species and habitat loss, the UN Environment report found.

The report is being released as climate experts and political and economic leaders seek to address dire findings released in October by the United Nations' Intergovernmental Panel on Climate Change, which urged rapid action to transform the global economy at a speed and scale that has "no documented historic precedent."

"This report solves the mystery of why problems such as pollution, declining biodiversity and climate change persist despite the proliferation of environmental laws in recent decades, "David Boyd, UN Special Rapporteur on Human Rights and the Environment said, " Unless the environmental rule of law is strengthened, even seemingly rigorous rules are destined to fail and the fundamental human right to a healthy environment will go unfulfilled."

"Dramatic Growth in Laws to Protect Environment, but Widespread Failure to Enforce, Finds Report," United Nations Environment Programme, January 24, 2019. Reprinted by permission.

While international aid did help countries to enter into over 1,100 environmental agreements since 1972 and develop many environmental framework laws, neither aid, nor domestic budgeting, has led to the establishment of strong environmental agencies capable of effectively enforcing laws and regulations. The report authors identify multiple factors contributing to poor enforcement of environmental rule of law, including poor coordination across government agencies, weak institutional capacity, lack of access to information, corruption and stifled civic engagement.

"We have the machinery in the form of laws, regulations and agencies to govern our environment sustainably," Joyce Msuya, Acting Executive Director of UN Environment said, " Political will is now critical to making sure our laws work for the planet. This first global assessment on environmental rule of law highlights the work of those standing on the right side of history — and how many nations are stronger and safer as a result."

The report details the many developments in environmental law since 1972, including the adoption of a constitutional right to a healthy environment by 88 countries, with another 65 countries having enshrined environmental protection in their constitutions. In addition, over 350 environmental courts and tribunals have been established in over 50 countries, and more than 60 countries have at least some legal provisions for citizens' right to environmental information.

"The international community can do more," Carl Bruch, Director of International Programs at the Environmental Law Institute said. "Too often donor support focuses on very specific areas of the environment, resulting in robust environmental programs in some areas, and no funding or attention to other areas. This patchwork approach can undermine environmental rule of law by not providing consistency in implementation and enforcement and by sending confusing messages to the regulated community and the public. As a result, many of these laws have yet to take root across society, and in most instances, the culture of environmental compliance is weak or non-existent."

The report devotes significant attention to one particularly worrying trend: the growing resistance to environmental laws, which has been most evident in the harassment, arbitrary arrests threats, and killing of environmental defenders. Between 2002 and 2013, 908 people — including forest rangers, government inspectors, and local activists — were killed in 35 countries, and in 2017 alone, 197 environmental defenders were murdered.

"The criminalization and increasing attacks on environment defenders are clear violations of environmental rule of law and an affront to the rights, roles and contributions of indigenous peoples and civil society in protecting our environment. This report captures the prevailing lack of accountability, strong environmental governance and respect for human rights for the sustainability of our environment," said Joan Carling, indigenous rights activist and environmental defender from the Philippines.

The effective engagement of an informed civil society results in better decision making by government, more responsible environmental actions by companies, and more effective environmental law. The provision of periodic reports on domestic environmental quality, including on air quality and water quality helps achieve these goals. Unfortunately, according to the Environmental Democracy Index, only 20 of 70 countries reviewed, or 28 percent, are ranked as "good" or "very good" in producing a regular, comprehensive, and current "State of the Environment" report. In India, Thailand, and Uganda, data on pollution stemming from industrial facilities can only be obtained through a personal contact.

Failure to Protect the Environment Will Have Negative Economic and Health Effects

Ryan Nunn, Jimmy O'Donnell, Jay Shambaugh,
Lawrence H. Goulder, Charles D. Kolstad, and
Xianling Long

Ryan Nunn is an assistant vice president for applied research in Community Development at the Federal Reserve Bank of Minneapolis. Jimmy O'Donnell is a senior research assistant with the Hamilton Project in the Economic Studies program at the Brookings Institution. Jay Shambaugh is a nonresident senior fellow in Economic Studies at the Brookings Institution. Lawrence H. Goulder and Charles D. Kolstad are senior fellows at the Stanford Institute for Economic Policy Research (SIEPR). Xianling Long is a research assistant at SIEPR.

The world's climate has already changed measurably in response to accumulating greenhouse gas (GHG) emissions. These changes as well as projected future disruptions have prompted intense research into the nature of the problem and potential policy solutions. This document aims to summarize much of what is known about both, adopting an economic lens focused on how ambitious climate objectives can be achieved at the lowest possible cost.

Considerable uncertainties surround both the extent of future climate change and the extent of the biophysical impacts of such change. Notwithstanding the uncertainties, climate scientists have reached a strong consensus that in the absence of measures to reduce GHG emissions significantly, the changes in climate will be substantial, with long-lasting effects on many of Earth's physical and biological systems. The central or median estimates of these impacts are significant. Moreover, there are significant

"Ten Facts About the Economics of Climate Change and Climate Policy," by Ryan Nunn, Jimmy O'Donnell, Jay Shambaugh, Lawrence H. Goulder, Charles D. Kolstad, and Xianling Long, The Brookings Institution, October 23, 2019. Reprinted by permission.

risks associated with low probability but potentially catastrophic outcomes. Although a focus on median outcomes alone warrants efforts to reduce emissions of GHGs, economists argue that the uncertainties and associated risks justify more aggressive policy action than otherwise would be warranted (Weitzman 2009; 2012).

The scientific consensus is expressed through summary documents offered every several years by the United Nations–sponsored Intergovernmental Panel on Climate Change (IPCC). These documents indicate the projected outcomes under alternative representative concentration pathways (RCPs) for GHGs (IPCC 2014). Each of these RCPs represents different GHG trajectories over the next century, with higher numbers corresponding to more emissions.

Representative Concentration Pathways (RCPs)

The expected path of GHG emissions is crucial to accurately forecasting the physical, biological, economic, and social effects of climate change. RCPs are scenarios, chosen by the IPCC, that represent scientific consensus on potential pathways for GHG emissions and concentrations, emissions of air pollutants, and land use through 2100. In their most-recent assessment, the IPCC selected four RCPs as the basis for its projections and analysis. We describe the RCPs and some of their assumptions below:

- RCP 2.6: emissions peak in 2020 and then decline through 2100.
- RCP 4.5: emissions peak between 2040 and 2050 and then decline through 2100.
- RCP 6.0: emissions continue to rise until 2080 and then decline through 2100.
- RCP 8.5: emissions rise continually through 2100.

The IPCC does not assign probabilities to these different emissions pathways. What is clear is that the pathways would require different changes in technology and policy. RCPs 2.6 and 4.5 would very likely require significant advances in technology and changes in policy in order to be realized. It seems highly unlikely that global emissions will follow the pathway outlined in RCP 2.6 in particular; annual emissions would have to start declining in 2020. By contrast, RCPs 6.0 and 8.5 represent scenarios in which future emissions follow past trends with minimal to no change in policy and/or technology.

The four RCPs imply different effects on global temperatures. [1] Only the significant reductions in emissions underlying RCPs 2.6 and 4.5 can stabilize average global temperature increases at or around 2°C. Many scientists have suggested that it is critical to avoid increases in temperature beyond 2°C or even 1.5°C— larger temperature increases would produce extreme biophysical impacts and associated human welfare costs. It is worth noting that economic assessments of the costs and benefits from policies to reduce CO_2 emissions do not necessarily recommend policies that would constrain temperature increases to 1.5°C or 2°C. Some economic analyses suggest that these temperature targets would be too stringent in the sense that they would involve economic sacrifices in excess of the value of the climate-related benefits (Nordhaus 2007, 2017). Other analyses tend to support these targets (Stern 2006). In scenarios with little or no policy action (RCPs 6.0 and 8.5), average global surface temperature could rise 2.9 to 4.3°C above preindustrial levels by the end of this century. One consequence of the temperature increase in these scenarios is that sea level would rise by between 0.5 and 0.8 meters.

Countries' Relative Contributions to CO_2 Emissions Are Changing

The extent of climate change is a function of the atmospheric stock of CO_2 and other greenhouse gases, and the stock at any given point in time reflects cumulative emissions up to that point. Thus, the contribution a given country or region makes to global climate change can be measured in terms of its cumulative emissions.

Up to 1990, the historical responsibility for climate change was primarily attributable to the more-industrialized countries. Between

1850 and 1990, the United States and Europe alone produced nearly 75 percent of cumulative CO_2 emissions. Such historic responsibility has been a primary issue in debates about how much of the burden of reducing current and future emissions should fall on the shoulders of developed versus developing countries.

Although the United States and other developed nations continue to be responsible for a large share of the current excess concentration of CO_2, relative contributions and responsibilities are changing. As of 2017, the United States and Europe accounted for just over 50 percent of cumulative CO_2 emitted into the atmosphere since 1850. A reason for this sharp decline is that CO_2 emissions from China, India, and other developing countries have grown faster than emissions from the developed countries (though amongst major economies, the United States has one of the highest rates of per capita emissions in the world and is far ahead of China and India [Joint Research Centre 2018]). Therefore, it seems likely that in order to avert the worst effects of climate change, emissions reduction efforts will be required by both historic contributors—the United States and Europe—as well as more recently developing countries such as China and India.

The future of climate change might seem dismal in light of the recent increase in global emissions as well as the potential future growth in emissions, temperatures, and sea levels under RCPs 6.0 and 8.5. Failure to take any climate policy action would lead to annual emissions growth rates far above those that would prevent temperature increases beyond the focal points of 1.5°C and 2°C. As indicated earlier, cost-benefit analyses in various economic models lead to differing conclusions as to whether it is optimal to constrain temperature increases to 1.5°C or 2°C (Nordhaus 2007, 2016; Stern 2006).[2] Fortunately, countries have been taking steps to combat climate change. Comparing "No climate policies" and "Current policy" shows that the emissions reduction implied by current policies will lead to roughly 1°C lower global temperature by the end of the century. A large share of this lowered emission path is attributable to actions by states, provinces, and municipalities throughout the world.

Further reductions are implied by the 2015 Paris Agreement, under which 195 countries pledged to take additional steps. The Paris Agreement's pledges, if met, would keep global temperatures 0.5°C lower than "Current policy" and about 1.5°C lower than "No climate policy" in 2100. Although this can be viewed as a positive outcome, a morenegative perspective is that these policies would still allow temperatures in 2100 to be 2.6 to 3.2°C above preindustrial levels—significantly above the 1.5 or 2.0°C targets that have become focal points in policy discussions.

In the following set of facts, we describe the costs of climate change to the United States and to the world as well as potential policy solutions and their respective costs.

Fact 1: Damages to the U.S. Economy Grow with Temperature Change at an Increasing Rate.

The physical changes described in the introduction will have substantial effects on the U.S. economy. Climate change will affect agricultural productivity, mortality, crime, energy use, storm activity, and coastal inundation (Hsiang et al. 2017).

It is immediately apparent that economic costs will vary greatly depending on the extent to which global temperature increase (above preindustrial levels) is limited by technological and policy changes. At 2°C of warming by 2080–99, Hsiang et al. (2017) project that the United States would suffer annual losses equivalent to about 0.5 percent of GDP in the years 2080–99. By contrast, if the global temperature increase were as large as 4°C, annual losses would be around 2.0 percent of GDP. Importantly, these effects become disproportionately larger as temperature rise increases: For the United States, rising mortality as well as changes in labor supply, energy demand, and agricultural production are all especially important factors in driving this nonlinearity.

Looking instead at per capita GDP impacts, Kahn et al. (2019) find that annual GDP per capita reductions (as opposed to economic costs more broadly) could be between 1.0 and 2.8 percent under IPCC's RCP 2.6, and under RCP 8.5 the range of losses could be between 6.7 and 14.3 percent. For context, in 2019 a 5 percent U.S. GDP loss would be roughly $1 trillion.

There is, of course, substantial uncertainty in these calculations. A major source of uncertainty is the extent of climate change over the next several decades, which depends largely on future policy choices and economic developments—both of which affect the level of total carbon emissions. As noted earlier, this uncertainty justifies more aggressive action to limit emissions and thereby help insure against the worst potential outcomes.

It is also important to highlight that economic effects that are not readily measurable are excluded, as are costs incurred by countries other than the United States. In addition, if climate change has an impact on the growth rate (as opposed to the level) of output in each year, then the impacts could compound to be much larger in the future (Dell, Jones, and Olken 2012).[3]

Fact 2: Struggling U.S. Counties Will Be Hit Hardest by Climate Change.

The effects of climate change will not be shared evenly across the United States; places that are already struggling will tend to be hit the hardest. To explore the local impacts of climate change, we use a summary measure of county economic vitality that incorporates labor market, income, and other data (Nunn, Parsons, and Shambaugh 2018), paired with county level costs as a share of GDP projected by Hsiang et al. (2017).[4]

The bottom fifth of counties ranked by economic vitality will experience the largest damages, with the bottom quintile of counties facing losses equal in value to nearly 7 percent of GDP in 2080–99 under the RCP 8.5 scenario (a projection that assumes little to no additional climate policy action and warming of roughly 4.3°C above preindustrial levels).[5] Counties that will be hit hardest by climate change tend to be located in the South and Southwest regions of the United States (Muro, Victor, and Whiton

2019). Rao (2017) finds that nearly two million homes are at risk of being underwater by 2100, with over half of those being located in Florida, Louisiana, North Carolina, South Carolina, and Texas. More-prosperous counties in the United States are often in the Northeast, upper Midwest, and Pacific regions, where temperatures are lower and communities are less exposed to climate damage.

An important limitation of these estimates is that they assume that population in each county remains constant over time (Hsiang et al. 2017).[6] To the extent that people will adjust to climate change by moving to less-vulnerable areas, this adjustment could help to diminish aggregate national damages but may exacerbate losses in places where employment falls. Moreover, the limited ability of low-income Americans to migrate in response to climate change exposes them to particular hardship (Kahn 2017).

The concentration of climate damages in the South and among low-income Americans implies a disproportionate impact on minority communities. Geographic disadvantage is overlaid with racial disadvantage (Hardy, Logan, and Parman 2018), and Black, Latino, and indigenous communities are likely to bear a disproportionate share of climate change burden (Gamble and Balbus 2016).

Fact 3: Globally, Low-Income Countries Will Lose Larger Shares of Their Economic Output.

Unlike other pollutants that have localized or regional effects, GHGs produce global effects. These emissions constitute a negative spillover at the widest scale possible: For example, emissions from the United States contribute to warming in China, and vice versa. Moreover, some places are much more exposed to economic damages from climate change than are other places; the same increase in atmospheric carbon concentration will cause larger per capita damages in India than in Iceland.

This means that carbon emissions and the damages from those emissions can be (and, in fact, are) distributed in very different ways. Impacts on per capita GDP based on a study of the GDP growth effects of warming, highlight the relatively high per capita income reductions in Latin America, Africa, and South Asia (though higher-income countries would lose more absolute aggregate wealth and output because of their higher levels of economic activity). A higher estimate of potential economic damages takes into account impacts on productivity and growth that accumulate over time as opposed to looking at snapshots of lost activity in a given year. Thus, the estimates are higher than those presented in facts 1 and 2, highlighting both the uncertainty and the potentially disastrous outcomes that are possible.

Fact 4: Increased Mortality from Climate Change Will Be Highest in Africa and the Middle East.

The reductions in economic output highlighted in fact 3 are not the only damages expected from climate change. One important example is the effect of climate change on mortality. In places that already experience high temperatures, climate change will exacerbate heat-related health issues and cause mortality rates to rise.

The geographical distribution of the impact on mortality is very uneven. Some of the most-significant impacts are in the equatorial zone because these locations are already very hot, and high temperatures become increasingly dangerous as temperatures rise further. For example, Accra, Ghana is projected to experience 160 additional deaths per 100,000 residents. In colder regions, mortality rates are sometimes predicted to fall, reflecting decreases in the number of dangerously cold days: Oslo, Norway is projected to experience 230 fewer deaths per 100,000. But for the world as a whole, negative effects are predominant, and on average 85 additional deaths per 100,000 will occur (Carleton et al. 2018).

Wealthier places are better able to protect themselves from the adverse consequences of climate change. This is a factor in projections of mortality risk from climate change: the bottom third of countries by income will experience almost all of the total increase in mortality rates (Carleton et al. 2018).

Mortality effects are disproportionately concentrated among the elderly population. This is true whether the effects are positive (when dangerously cold days are reduced) or negative (when dangerously hot days are increased) (Carleton et al. 2018; Deschenes and Moretti 2009).

Fact 5: Energy Intensity and Carbon Intensity Have Been Falling in the U.S. Economy.

The high-damage climate outcomes described in previous facts are not inevitable: There are good reasons to believe that substantial emissions reductions are attainable. For example, not only has the emissions-to-GDP ratio of the U.S. economy declined over the past two decades, but during the last decade the absolute level of emissions has declined as well, despite the growth of the economy. From a peak in 2007 through 2017, U.S. carbon emissions have fallen 14 percent while output grew 16 percent (Bureau of Economic Analysis 2007–17; U.S. Environmental Protection Agency [EPA] 2007–17; authors' calculations). This reversal was produced by a combination of declining energy intensity of the U.S. economy and declining carbon intensity of U.S. energy use. However, emissions increased in 2018, which suggests that sound policy will be needed to continue making progress (Rhodium Group 2019).

U.S. energy intensity (defined as energy consumed per dollar of GDP) has been falling both in times of economic expansion and contraction, allowing the economy to grow even as energy use falls. This has been crucial for mitigating climate change damages (CEA 2017; Obama 2017). Some estimates suggest that declining energy intensity has been the biggest contributor to U.S. reductions in carbon emissions (EIA 2018). Technological advancements and energy efficiency improvements have in turn driven the reduction in energy intensity (Metcalf 2008; Sue Wing 2008).

At the same time that energy intensity has fallen, the carbon intensity of energy use has also fallen in each of the major sectors. Improved methods for horizontal drilling have led to substantial increases in the supply of low-cost natural gas and less use of (relatively carbon-intensive) coal (CEA 2017).[7] Technological advances have also helped substantially reduce the cost of providing power from renewable energy sources like wind and solar. From 2008 to 2015, roughly two thirds of falling carbon intensity in the power sector came from using cleaner fossil fuels and one third from an increased use of renewables (CEA 2017). Non-hydro-powered renewable energy has risen substantially over a short period of time, from 4 percent of all net electricity generation in 2009 to 10 percent in 2018 (EIA 2019a; authors' calculations).

Fact 6: The Price of Renewable Energy Is Falling.

The declining cost of producing renewable energy has played a key role in the trends described in fact 5. Because these price decreases have followed largely from technology induced supply increases, solar and wind energy now play a more-important role in the U.S. energy mix (CEA 2017). In many settings, however, clean energy remains more expensive on average than fossil fuels (The Hamilton Project [THP] and the Energy Policy Institute at the University of Chicago [EPIC] 2017), highlighting the need for continued technological advances.

The increasing share of renewables in energy supply is due in part to cost-reducing advances in technology and increased exploitation of economies of scale. Government subsidies—justified by the social costs of carbon emissions—for renewable energy have also played a role. When the negative spillovers from CO_2 emissions are incorporated into the price of fossil fuels, many forms of clean energy are far cheaper than many fossil fuels (THP and EPIC 2017). However, making a much broader use of clean energy faces technological hurdles that have not yet been fully addressed. Renewable energy sources are in many cases intermittent—they make power only when the wind blows or the sun shines—and shifting towards more renewable energy production may require substantial improvements in battery technology and changes to how the electricity market prices variability (CEA 2016). The technological developments that drive falling clean energy prices are the product of public and private investments. In a Hamilton Project policy proposal, David Popp (2019) examines ways to encourage faster development and deployment of clean energy technologies.

Fact 7: Some Emissions Abatement Approaches Are Much More Costly Than Others.

There are many ways to reduce net carbon emissions, from better livestock management to renewable fuel subsidies to reforestation. Each of these abatement strategies comes with its own costs and benefits. To facilitate comparisons, researchers have calculated the cost per ton of CO_2-equivalent emissions.[8] [9]

Less-expensive programs and policies include the Clean Power Plan—a since-discontinued 2014 initiative to reduce power sector emissions—as well as methane flaring regulations and reforestation. By contrast, weatherization assistance and the vehicle trade-in policy Cash for Clunkers are more expensive. It is important to recognize that some policies may have goals other than emissions abatement, as with Cash for Clunkers, which also aimed to provide fiscal stimulus after the Great Recession (Li, Linn, and Spiller 2013; Mian and Sufi 2012).

But when the goal is to reduce emissions at the lowest cost, economic theory and common sense suggest that the cheapest strategies for abating emissions should be implemented first. State and federal policy choices can play an important role in determining which of the options are implemented and in what order.

A common approach is to impose certain emissions standards— for example, a low-carbon fuel standard. The difficulty with this approach is that, in some cases, standards require abatement methods involving relatively high costs per ton while some low-cost methods are not implemented. This can reflect government regulators' limited information about abatement costs or political pressures that favor some standards over others. By contrast, a carbon price—discussed in facts 8 through 10—helps to achieve a given emissions reduction target at the minimum cost by encouraging abatement actions that cost less than the carbon price and discouraging actions that cost more than that price.

However, policies other than a carbon price are often worthy of consideration. In a Hamilton Project proposal, Carolyn Fischer describes the situations in which clean performance standards can be implemented in a relatively efficient manner (2019).[10]

Fact 8: Numerous Carbon Pricing Initiatives Have Been Introduced Worldwide, and the Prices Vary Significantly.

At the local, national, and international levels, 57 carbon pricing programs have been implemented or are scheduled for implementation across the world (World Bank 2019).

By imposing a cost on emissions, a carbon price encourages activities that can reduce emissions at a cost less than the carbon price.

Immediately apparent is the wide range of the carbon prices, reflecting the range of carbon taxes and aggregate emissions caps that different governments have introduced. At the highest end is Sweden with its price of $126 per ton; by contrast, Poland and Ukraine have imposed prices just above zero.[11] A sufficiently high carbon price would change the cost-benefit assessment of some existing nonprice policies, as described in a Hamilton Project proposal by Roberton Williams (2019).

A crucial question for policy is the appropriate level of a carbon price. According to economic theory, efficiency is maximized when the carbon price is equal to the social cost of carbon.[12] In other words, a carbon price at that level would not only facilitate the adoption of the lowest-cost abatement activities (as discussed under fact 7) but would also achieve the level of overall emissions abatement that maximizes the difference between the climate-related benefits and the economic costs.[13] Although setting the carbon price equal to the social cost of carbon maximizes net benefits, the monetized environmental benefits also exceed the economic costs when the carbon price is below (or somewhat above) the optimal value.

Estimates of the social cost of carbon depend on a wide range of factors, including the projected biophysical impacts associated with an incremental ton of CO_2 emissions, the monetized value of these impacts, and the discount rate applied to convert future monetized damages into current dollars.[14] As of 2016, the Interagency Working Group on Social Cost of Carbon—a partnership of U.S. government agencies—reported a focal estimate of the social cost of carbon (SCC) at $51 (adjusted for inflation to 2018 dollars) per ton of CO_2.[15]

Fact 9: Most Global GHG Emissions Are Still Not Covered by a Carbon Pricing Initiative.

Just as important as the carbon price is the share of global emissions facing the price. Many countries do not price carbon, and in many of the countries that do, important sources of emissions are not covered. When implementing carbon prices, policymakers have tended to start with the power sector and exclude some other emissions sources like energy-intensive manufacturing (Fischer 2019).

The carbon pricing systems that do exist are not evenly distributed across the world (World Bank 2019). Programs are heavily concentrated in Europe, Asia, and, to a lesser extent, North America. This distribution aligns roughly with the distribution of emissions, though the United States is an outlier: as discussed in the introduction, Europe has generated 33 percent of global CO_2 emissions since 1850, the United States 25 percent, and China 13 percent (Ritchie and Roser 2017; authors' calculations). According to currently scheduled and implemented initiatives, in 2020 the United States will be pricing only 1.0 percent of global GHG emissions; by comparison, Europe will be pricing 5.5 percent, and China will be pricing 7.0 percent.

Between 2005 and 2012, the European Union's cap and trade program was the only major carbon pricing program. However since the Paris Agreement, there has been a growing number of implemented and scheduled programs, with the largest of these being China's national cap and trade program set to take effect in 2020. Despite this activity, it is likely that a carbon price will still not be applied to 80 percent of global emissions of GHGs in 2020 (World Bank 2019; authors' calculations).

Fact 10: Proposed U.S. Carbon Taxes Would Yield Significant Reductions in CO_2 and Environmental Benefits in Excess of the Costs.

To assess proposals for a national U.S. carbon price, it is important to understand the size of the likely emissions reduction. Over the 2020-30 period a carbon tax starting at $25 per ton in 2020 and increasing at 1 percent annually above the rate of inflation achieves a reduction in CO_2 of 10.5 gigatons, or an 18 percent reduction from the baseline (emissions level in 2005). A more-ambitious $50 per ton price, rising at 5 percent subsequently, would reduce near-term emissions by an estimated 30 percent.[16]

A major attraction of using carbon pricing to achieve emissions reductions (as compared to adopting standards and other conventional regulations for this purpose) is its ability to induce the market to adopt the lowest-cost methods for reducing emissions. As of late 2019, nine U.S. states participate in the Regional Greenhouse Gas Initiative (RGGI), in which electric power plants trade permits that currently have a market price of around $5.20 per short ton of carbon 10. Proposed U.S. carbon taxes would yield significant reductions in CO_2 and environmental benefits in excess of the costs. (RGGI Inc. 2019).[17] That means that electric power plants covered under the RGGI are able to find methods of emissions abatement at a cost of $5.20 per ton at the margin and would buy permits at that price rather than undertake any abatement opportunities at a higher cost. A lower aggregate cap—or a higher carbon tax—would continue to select for the abatement approaches that have the lowest costs per ton for a given sector.

Even at much higher levels, emissions pricing leads to environmental benefits—reduced climate and other environmental damages—that exceed the economic sacrifices involved (i.e., the expense of reducing emissions).[18] A central estimate of the social cost of carbon (in 2018 dollars) is $51 per ton (Interagency Working Group on Social Cost of Carbon 2016). However, many recent proposals have tended to entail carbon prices below this level.[19] Goulder and Hafstead (2017) find that a U.S. carbon tax of $20 per ton in 2019, increasing at 4 percent in real terms for 20 years after that, yields climate related benefits that exceed the economic costs by about 70 percent.[20]

Endnotes

1. Each RCP embodies a different set of assumptions about emissions, as described in box 1. Each RCP was also formulated by a different modeling team drawing on different elements of the research literature. As such, the parameters of each RCP are not fully harmonized, and the range of RCP projections reflects both different modeling assumptions and different assumptions about emissions.

2. It should be noted that some scenarios used to make emissions projections are not RCPs. Instead, they use policy scenarios outlined by the Climate Action Tracker.

3. It remains an open question whether climate change will principally affect the level or the growth rate of economic output.

4. The vitality index is a measure of a county's economic and social health based on a number of factors, including median household income, the poverty rate, life expectancy, the prime-age employment-to-population rate, housing vacancy rates, and the unemployment rate. Quintiles are weighted by county population. For more, see Nunn, Parsons, and Shambaugh (2018).

5. Some researchers regard the RCP 8.5 scenario as unlikely to occur (Raftery et al. 2017). The estimates of damages in figure 2 should in that case be thought of as an upper bound for the costs that Hsiang et al. (2017) consider.

6. Hsiang et al. (2017) also assume a limited degree of adaptation to climate change, accounting for adaptive responses currently observed but not those that might be introduced in response to more dramatic climate change.

7. Natural gas has increased its share of total electricity generation from 23.3 percent in 2009 to 35.1 percent in 2018, building on a cost advantage and the discovery of new gas sources (EIA 2019a; authors' calculations).

8. Some greenhouse gases, such as methane, have different consequences for the climate and must be translated into CO_2-equivalent units in order to compile an overall assessment of emissions. (Gillingham and Stock 2018)

9. Note that marginal abatement costs—the expense of removing one additional ton of carbon—may be higher or lower than the average abatement costs (Gillingham and Stock 2018).

10. For example, Fischer (2019) shows that when it is not possible to price emissions associated with imports, a domestic carbon price might simply divert carbon emissions to foreign countries; policies like tradable performance standards can abate emissions while avoiding this outcome.

11. In some cases, policymakers intend to start with a low price and gradually increase it, allowing for a more gradual transition. In other cases, high prices are combined with other design features that can lessen their impact on industry: for example, Sweden's high price is paired with output-based rebates (see Fischer 2019 for discussion of output-based rebates).

12. Economic analyses indicate that in the presence of distortionary taxes, the optimal carbon tax rate is 8–24 percent lower than it would be in their absence (Bovenberg and Goulder 1996; Barrage, forthcoming).

13. Another basis for setting the carbon price is in terms of the necessary level for achieving countries' Paris Agreement commitments; the World Bank has estimated that this requires a carbon price between $40 and $80 per ton (World Bank 2019).

14. See National Academies of Sciences, Engineering, and Medicine (2017) for an extensive discussion.

15. They reported a range of estimates depending on the discount rate used, including $75.27 for a 2.5 percent discount rate or $14.57 for a 5 percent discount rate. Reflecting the possibility of a catastrophic outcome, they also reported the 95th percentile estimate using the 3 percent discount rate of $149.33. More recently, the Trump administration decided to count only domestic costs in calculating the SCC, substantially lowering it. In addition, the administration chose to use the discount rates in standard cost benefit analysis of 3 percent and 7 percent rather than using 2.5, 3, and 5 percent as a range of discount rates. Many economists have argued that for very long time horizons it is important to use lower discount rates or a declining discount rate (Weitzman 1998). A discount rate of 7 percent implies that $100 of damages 100 years in the future is only worth spending $0.08 to avoid today, while a discount rate of 2.5 percent would say it is worth $8.00 to avoid the damage.

16 In addition to reduced climate change damages, the carbon tax also yields non-climate environmental benefits by causing reductions in local air pollutants, including nitrogen oxide, particulate matter, and sulfur dioxide. These reductions imply benefits to human health. Many studies find that these co-benefits are quantitatively as important as the climate benefits. Local pollution benefits are about 50 percent greater than the climate benefits (Goulder and Hafstead 2017). When the co-benefits are included, the carbon tax's benefits exceed its costs by a factor of four.

17. A short ton is equivalent to 0.907185 metric tons.

18. A carbon tax would have different effects on different groups of households. Those that consume more carbon-intense products may face higher costs. This

works toward a regressive effect, whereby the impact as a share of income is larger for low-income households. However, recent empirical studies point out other channels that work in the opposite direction. In particular, when some (or all) of the carbon tax revenue is rebated on a per capita basis, the overall impact is progressive and the policy has a positive impact on the average low-income household (Goulder et al. 2019; Metcalf, forthcoming).

19. Several recent proposals recommend initial rates around $25 per ton. They include the Climate Action Rebate Act, the Health Climate and Family Security Act, the Market Choice Act, and the American Opportunity Carbon Fee Act.

20. This is based on a time path for the SCC that starts at $42 per ton and increases at a rate of between 1 and 2 percent per year. The SCC follows the time path from the Interagency Working Group report prepared during the Obama administration (Interagency Working Group on Social Cost of Carbon 2016).

Self-Regulation Can Be Good for Companies and Consumers

Scott Shackelford

Scott Shackelford is an associate professor at the Indiana University Kelley School of Business, where he teaches cybersecurity law and policy, sustainability, and international business. He is also Director of the Ostrom Workshop Program on Cybersecurity and Internet Governance at Indiana University.

If Boeing is allowed to certify that a crash-prone aircraft is safe, and Facebook can violate users' privacy expectations, should companies and industries ever be allowed to police themselves? The debate is heating up particularly in the U.S. tech sector with growing calls to regulate—or even break up—the likes of Google, Apple and Amazon.

It turns out to be possible, at least sometimes, for companies and industries to govern themselves, while still protecting the public interest. Groundbreaking work by Nobel Prize-winning political economist Elinor Ostrom and her husband Vincent found a solution to a classic economic quandary, in which people—and businesses—self-interestedly enrich themselves as quickly as possible with certain resources including personal data, thinking little about the secondary costs they might be inflicting on others.

As the director of the Ostrom Workshop Program on Cybersecurity and Internet Governance, I have been involved in numerous projects studying how to solve these sorts of problems when they arise, both online and offline. Most recently, my work has looked at how to manage the massively interconnected world of sensors, computers and smart devices—what I and others call the "internet of everything."

"Companies' Self-Regulation Doesn't Have to Be Bad for the Public," by Scott Shackelford, The Conversation Media Group Ltd, June 12, 2019. https://theconversation.com/companies-self-regulation-doesnt-have-to-be-bad-for-the-public-117565. Licensed under CC BY-ND 4.0.

I've found that there are ways companies can become leaders by experimenting with business opportunities and collaborating with peers, while still working with regulators to protect the public, including both in the air and in cyberspace.

Tragedy Revisited

In a classic economic problem, called "the tragedy of the commons," a parcel of grassland is made available for a community to graze its livestock. Everyone tries to get the most benefit from it—and as a result, the land is overgrazed. What started as a resource for everyone becomes of little use to anyone.

For many years, economists thought there were only two possible solutions. One was for the government to step in and limit how many people could graze their animals. The other was to split the land up among private owners who had exclusive use of it, and could sustainably manage it for their individual benefit.

The Ostroms, however, found a third way. In some cases, they revealed, self-organization can work well, especially when the various people and groups involve can communicate effectively. They called it "polycentric governance," because it allows regulation to come from more than just one central authority. Their work can help determine if and when companies can effectively regulate themselves—or whether it's best for the government to step in.

A Polycentric Primer

The concept can seem complicated, but in practice it is increasingly popular, in federal programs and even as a goal for governing the internet.

Scholars such as Elinor Ostrom produced a broad swath of research over decades, looking at public schools and police department performance in Midwestern U.S. cities, coastal overfishing, forest management in nations like Nepal, and even traffic jams in New York City. They identified commonalities among all these studies, including whether the group's members can help set the rules by which their shared resources are governed, how much control they have over who gets to share it, how disputes are resolved, and how everyone's use is monitored.

All of these factors can help predict whether individuals or groups will successfully self-regulate, whether the challenge they're facing is climate change, cybersecurity, or anything else. Trust is key, as Lin Ostrom said, and an excellent way to build trust is to let smaller groups make their own decisions.

Polycentric governance's embrace of self-regulation involves relying on human ingenuity and collaboration skills to solve difficult problems—while focusing on practical measures to address specific challenges.

Self-regulation does have its limits, though—as has been clear in the revelations about how the Federal Aviation Administration allowed Boeing to certify the safety of its own software. Facebook has also been heavily criticized for failing to block an anonymous horde of users across the globe from manipulating people's political views.

Polycentric regulation is a departure from the idea of "keep it simple, stupid"—rather, it is a call for engagement by numerous groups to grapple with the complexities of the real world.

Both Facebook and Boeing now need to convince themselves, their employees, investors, policymakers, users and customers that they can be trusted. Ostrom's ideas suggest they could begin to do this by engaging with peers and industry groups to set rules and ensure they are enforced.

Governing the "Internet of Everything"

Another industry in serious need of better regulations is the smart-device business, with tens of billions of connected devices around the world, and little to no concern for user security or privacy.

Customers often buy the cheapest smart-home camera or digital sensor, without looking at competitors' security and privacy protections. The results are predictable—hackers have hijacked thousands of internet-connected devices and used them to attack the physical network of the internet, take control of industrial equipment, and spy on private citizens through their smartphones and baby monitors.

Some governments are starting to get involved. The state of California and the European Union are exploring laws that promote "reasonable" security requirements, at least as a baseline. The EU is encouraging companies to band together to establish industry-wide codes of conduct.

Getting Governance Right

Effective self-governance may seem impossible in the "Internet of everything" because of the scale and variety of groups and industries involved, but polycentric governance does provide a useful lens through which to view these problems. Ostrom has asserted this approach may be the most flexible and adaptable way to manage rapidly changing industries. It may also help avoid conflicting government regulations that risk stifling innovation in the name of protecting consumers without helping either cause.

But success is not certain. It requires active engagement by all parties, who must share a sense of responsibility to the customers and mutual trust in one another. That's not easy to build in any community, let alone the dynamic tech industry.

Government involvement can help build bridges and solidify trust across the private sector, as happened with cybersecurity efforts from the National Institute for Standards and Technology. Some states, like Ohio, are even rewarding firms for using appropriate self-regulation in their cybersecurity decision-making.

Polycentric governance can be flexible, adapting to new technologies more appropriately—and often more quickly—than pure governmental regulation. It also can be more efficient and cost-effective, though it's not a cure for all regulatory ills. And it's important to note that regulation can spur innovation as well as protect consumers, especially when the rules are simple and outcome focused.

Consider the North American Electric Reliability Council. That organization was originally created as a group of companies that came together voluntarily in an effort to protect against blackouts. NERC standards, however, were eventually made legally enforceable in the aftermath of the Northeast blackout of 2003. They are an example of an organic code of conduct that was voluntarily adopted and subsequently reinforced by government, consistent with professor Ostrom's ideas. Ideally, it should not require such a crisis to spur this process forward.

Ultimately, what's needed—and what professor Ostrom and her colleagues and successors have called for—is more experimentation and less theorizing. As the 10-year anniversary of Ostrom's Nobel Prize approaches, I believe it is time to put her insights to work, offering industries the opportunity to self-regulate where appropriate while leaving the door open for the possibility of government action, including antitrust enforcement, to protect the public and promote cyber peace.

Overregulation Stifles Growth and Innovation

Lalit Bhasin

Lalit Bhasin is the regional president of the Indo-American Chamber of Commerce, which promotes trade and investment between India and the US. He has also worked as a lawyer and managing partner at Bhasin and Company in New Delhi, India.

With sales numbers from the recently concluded e-commerce sale season belying the perceived economic slowdown, the e-commerce sector's resilience indicates an increasingly sharper understanding of what both India and Bharat want. For this, India's e-commerce industry deserves kudos.

In this context, it was surprising to hear that the government's department for promotion of investment and internal trade (DPIIT) has asked these e-commerce marketplaces for a host of details, mostly investigative in nature. Along with looking into the volume of business, investments, commission agreements, and lists of sellers and distributors, the DPIIT has asked them to confirm compliance with rules relating to the goods and services tax in letter and spirit. The timing of these requests, and their nature, covering capital structure details, business models and inventory management systems, raise a simple question: Is the value derived from e-commerce's co-existence with traditional businesses being undermined because of the fear of a business model that benefits all but is still seen by some as a threat?

That value has several dimensions. The foremost is e-commerce's impact on India's 12 million kirana stores. Accounting for 88% of the country's total retail market revenues, these neighbourhood shops have an unparalleled ability to serve hyper-local needs. This is also the basis of the e-commerce-kirana win-win proposition. While kirana stores enable the online marketplace to excel in

"Opinion: Over-Regulation of E-Commerce Could Stifle Its Growth," by Lalit Bhasin, Livemint, October 30, 2019. Reprinted by permission.

helping products reach last-mile destinations in hinterland markets, they benefit from the extra revenue stream that comes from this partnership. Kirana shops also benefit as they can adopt international best practices for better management of their inventory and the expansion of their reach. Kirana outlets and e-commerce can go hand in hand, and their joint strength can result in significant job creation in line with the government's policy and skill development goals.

It also must be noted that amid a perceived nationwide slowdown in consumption, India's e-commerce sector has recorded its highest sales ever. Notably, a significant chunk of the ₹19,000 crore gross merchandise value across the six-day festive sale run by online platforms came from small-town India. This indicates that e-commerce is generating sufficient value for all buyer classes, enabling it to boost consumption in a way that is both exponential and inclusive. A plethora of product sellers are getting access to e-commerce marketplaces that could have been difficult to tap, thus giving them greater reason to participate. The fact that e-commerce majors have regularly reiterated their vision of drawing more Indian buyers and sellers into their fold, with both seeking to make the most of rising mobile penetration and favourable demographics, speaks well of its future prospects.

The potential of job creation in e-commerce is evident from the extent to which it has penetrated India's retail and consumption ecosystem. As it sustains its growth trajectory, e-commerce can emerge as a leading generator of jobs in areas ranging from delivery, logistics and data-analytics to product and brand experience, design and inventory management, as well as support functions such as finance, payments, legal and human resources. Newer and more specialised competencies, including payment gateways, big data and mobile technology are being harnessed to give consumers a hassle-free purchase experience.

It should also be appreciated that e-commerce today is not a monolith. The sector comprises a growing number of players of various sizes. To remain competitive, they will all have to make regular investments that would place our workforce on a par with its global counterparts, while also serving to acquire and sustain a business advantage that enables the sector to surge ahead.

Having whetted India's purchase palate, e-commerce is giving equal shelf space to domestic artisans and small- and medium-sized manufacturers, granting them access to local, national and even global markets. As the e-commerce sector grows and deepens, its engagement with both the "classes" and the "masses" of India, so to speak, its status as a multiplier of prosperity, can only grow.

India's e-commerce sector has benefited from a pro-business policy environment. It is where it is today, to an extent, on account of government initiatives such as Digital India, Skill India, Startup India and Make in India. Today, placed at the intersection of economic growth, job creation and unprecedented market access for enterprises of all sizes, the e-commerce growth story epitomizes the inclusiveness of the Indian economy set in motion by government policies.

While strategically designed and implemented regulations have a place in our economy, being overly critical of a marketplace that currently serves as a beacon of commercial success may inadvertently stifle its growth and bring back the worst of the Licence Raj regime. The sector's multifaceted positives and its evolving nature have led the government to adopt a consultative approach. Such consultations must continue. As one of the fastest growing online retail markets among the economies of the world, the sector must be assured of a fair policy framework to support India's emergence as a $5 trillion economy by fiscal year 2024-25.

Consumers Pay a High Price for Regulation

Sam Batkins

Sam Batkins is the former director of regulatory policy for American Action Forum (AAF), a nonprofit conservative issue advocacy group based in Washington, DC. He now works as the director of strategy and research at Mastercard.

Amerian Action Forum (AAF) research finds that 36 regulations issued during the Obama Administration will increase consumer prices by more than $11,000. From higher priced vehicles, pricier household goods, to more expensive food, the cumulative effect of regulation has profound implications for consumers and the broader economy.

Methodology

AAF reviewed all recent "economically significant" regulations (rules with an annual impact on the economy of greater than $100 million) to determine whether the agency's regulatory impact analyses concluded that the regulation would raise prices. Although more than 50 rules determined that the regulation would impact consumers, AAF found only 36 that quantified those impacts.

For example, the Environmental Protection Agency (EPA) and the National Highway Traffic Safety Administration (NHTSA) acknowledge that consumer prices will increase from recent vehicle efficiency standards. In just one of the earlier rules, for Model Year 2011 vehicles, NHTSA admitted passenger cars and light truck prices would increase by $91.

AAF recorded any instance of an agency quantifying consumer price increases and then divided these increases into six areas:

- Vehicles: $9,150
- Household Consumer Products: $1,639

"The Consumer Price of Regulation", by Sam Batkins, The American Action Forum, May 27, 2014. Reprinted by permission.

- Mortgage: $362 (annual)
- Energy: $135 (annual)
- Health Care: $108 (annual)
- Food: $14 (annual)

From these six areas, AAF estimated the increased cost a consumer would pay because of the regulation. For some regulations, analyses simply listed the price increase. For others, namely energy efficiency standards, AAF had to compare the average installed price of new units to the baseline, pre-regulation cost. In instances where a regulation controlled several different product classes, AAF averaged these cost increases. Sofie Miller's work at the GW Regulatory Studies Center also supplemented the research on increasing product prices.

Results

Overall Regulatory Price Increases by Sector, Excluding Vehicles

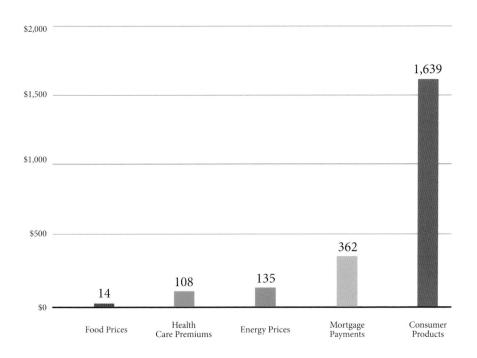

Consumer Products

This class had the largest number of covered products: from dishwashers ($44 increase), to clothes washers ($18 increase) and refrigerators ($83 increase), there are few electronic household devices that have not been regulated recently. The administration has finalized more than a dozen "economically significant" Department of Energy regulations during the past five years. Many of these measures admit consumers will pay higher prices, but if purchasers keep goods for a certain "payback period," lower energy costs will result in net gains.

Combined, regulations will increase the cost of consumer goods by up to $1,600. Below are the more notable items that consumers can expect to pay higher prices for in the future.

- Fluorescent Lamps: $1.80
- Microwave Ovens: $14
- Air Conditioners: $320
- Dishwashers: $44

Food

There are four notable regulations that will force consumers to pay more at the grocery store. The largest by far, is the result of the renewable fuel standard. According to an EPA analysis, higher commodity prices would increase food prices by "roughly $10 per person per year." Combined, four recent regulations will increase food prices by approximately $14, including higher prices for eggs and sugar.

Mortgages

Increasing the cost of a mortgage is the most glaring area where agencies provided only qualitative analysis or simply omitted any extensive discussion of how regulation could increase costs. AAF found only two rules, out of hundreds of Dodd-Frank and other notable rules, which explicitly mentioned they could increase mortgage costs. The largest, "Appraisals for Higher-Risk

Mortgage Loans," requires creditors to obtain an appraisal and provide applicants a copy of written home appraisals. The agencies estimated this appraisal would cost roughly $350 and could be passed on to consumers.

The other notable rule increasing mortgage costs is actually from EPA. The rule, Effluent Limitations Guidelines, could increase monthly mortgages from $1 to $29, depending on the regulatory alternative. AAF used the $1 figure; thus, annual mortgage costs increase by $12, for a combined $362 increase for these two rules.

Energy Prices

EPA has also "missed the forest for the trees" in its analysis of recent power sector regulations. Although it has acknowledged that some of its rules could increase utility bills, the agency has always been careful to note price spikes are "small relative to the changes observed in the absolute levels of electricity prices over the last 50 years." However, when combined with four other regulations, variations are no longer trivial. For one rule, "Utility MACT," the price increase was 3.1 percent.

EPA also issued the Cross-State Air Pollution Rule (CSPAR), which could increase retail electricity prices "by about 1.7 percent." Although the 3.1 percent spike from Utility MACT might seem trivial, with CSAPR, consumers could now face a 4.8 percent increase. During the year, the average consumer could pay approximately $71 more in energy costs because of these two rules.

However, that's not the end of high energy prices. EPA recently finalized its Tier 3 emission standard rule, which would lower the sulfur content in gasoline to 10 parts per million, from 30 parts per million. The agency noted it would slightly increase vehicle prices (noted below), but it would also impose costs on refiners, which would then be passed on in the form of higher gasoline prices. The price increase is less than a cent per gallon, but the per capita impact during the year is roughly $3.00. In total, consumers can expect to pay $135 annually in higher energy prices from just a handful of recent rules.

Health Care

Two Affordable Care Act rules, coverage for preventive services and preexisting conditions, will increase annual premiums by more than $87. In the preventive services rule, the administration conceded that, "Premiums will increase by approximately 1.5 percent on average." In the preexisting conditions rule, the administration admitted premium increases could vary from 0.2 percent to as high as 6.6 percent. The average projected increase was 1.9 percent, the figure AAF used to calculate the $49 annual impact of the rule.

Finally, a 2013 rule implementing the Mental Health Parity Act is also likely to increase premiums. According to the administration, new coverage "could be expected to lead to an increase of 0.8 percent in premiums." Combined with the 1.9 percent and 1.5 percent increases in other rules, patients now face premium increases of 4.2 percent. This represents just three regulations out of dozens that have the potential to raise prices. Combined, these rules will increase annual premiums by more than $108.

Vehicles

In total, 36 recent regulations increased consumer prices by more than $11,100. For vehicles, prices jumped by more than $9,100, the vast majority of the sample's increase. The $9,100 figure includes three major rounds of fuel efficiency standards, which increased prices by approximately $2,800. It also includes three safety standards, which added $287, and Tier 3 sulfur emissions standards, which will contribute $72 to higher vehicle prices. However, the largest increase, $6,000, is from a "typical combination truck/tractor." An average consumer will be forced to pay more than $3,100 for a vehicle due to regulation, but some consumers could spend far more because of these new rules.

Implications

Beyond higher prices for consumers, the broader economy is also affected by increased regulatory spending. For example, price increases generally result in decreased sales, affecting manufacturers and consumers.

In EPA's most recent fuel efficiency regulations, the agency concluded, "There is broad consensus in the economic literature that the price elasticity for demand for automobiles is approximately -1.0." Thus, a one percent increase in vehicle prices results in a one percent decrease in sales. A combined $3,100 price hike for vehicles could decrease vehicle sales by up to ten percent, resulting in billions of dollars in lost sales and fewer jobs.

For energy, the elasticities are slightly less than they are for automobiles: the National Energy Modeling System concludes a "1 percent increase in prices leads to a 0.1 to 0.3 percent decrease in energy demand." For Utility MACT and CSAPR alone, a 4.8 percent increase in energy prices could result in a 1.4 percent reduction in energy demand.

Vehicle Regulation Price Increases, Excluding Heavy-Duty Trucks

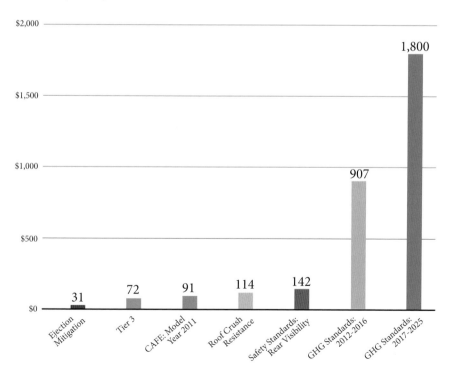

Beyond higher consumer prices and lessening demand, there is a possibility that consumers won't want the newly regulated products, either because of price or preference. The Department of Energy noted that new light bulbs "may result in consumers' unwillingness to purchase them." Consumers also might simply continue to use their less efficient current products, rather that purchasing more expensive items. For CAFE, economists Mark Jacobsen and Arthur van Benthem estimate 13 to 23 percent of "the expected fuel savings will leak away through the used vehicle market. This considerably reduces the cost-effectiveness of the standard."

Conclusion

$11,000 in higher consumer prices is a striking figure, but this represents just 36 recent rules. In addition, federal agencies provided all the data and there are certainly higher outside estimates. Regardless of the final figure, it's clear that federal regulations increase prices for every consumer. Although companies typically comply with new rules, consumers must often pay the bill.

CHAPTER 4

Is It Possible for Consumption to Become More Sustainable?

Overview: Convenient Consumption Isn't Always Sustainable Consumption

Science History Institute

The Science History Institute is a Philadelphia-based institution that preserves and interprets the history of science. It comprises a museum, library, and research center.

Plastic is a word that originally meant "pliable and easily shaped." It only recently became a name for a category of materials called polymers. The word polymer means "of many parts," and polymers are made of long chains of molecules. Polymers abound in nature. Cellulose, the material that makes up the cell walls of plants, is a very common natural polymer.

Over the last century and a half humans have learned how to make synthetic polymers, sometimes using natural substances like cellulose, but more often using the plentiful carbon atoms provided by petroleum and other fossil fuels. Synthetic polymers are made up of long chains of atoms, arranged in repeating units, often much longer than those found in nature. It is the length of these chains, and the patterns in which they are arrayed, that make polymers strong, lightweight, and flexible. In other words, it's what makes them so plastic.

These properties make synthetic polymers exceptionally useful, and since we learned how to create and manipulate them, polymers have become an essential part of our lives. Especially over the last 50 years plastics have saturated our world and changed the way that we live.

The First Synthetic Plastic

The first synthetic polymer was invented in 1869 by John Wesley Hyatt, who was inspired by a New York firm's offer of $10,000 for anyone who could provide a substitute for ivory. The growing

"History and Future of Plastics," Science History Institute. Reprinted by permission.

popularity of billiards had put a strain on the supply of natural ivory, obtained through the slaughter of wild elephants. By treating cellulose, derived from cotton fiber, with camphor, Hyatt discovered a plastic that could be crafted into a variety of shapes and made to imitate natural substances like tortoiseshell, horn, linen, and ivory.

This discovery was revolutionary. For the first time human manufacturing was not constrained by the limits of nature. Nature only supplied so much wood, metal, stone, bone, tusk, and horn. But now humans could create new materials. This development helped not only people but also the environment. Advertisements praised celluloid as the savior of the elephant and the tortoise. Plastics could protect the natural world from the destructive forces of human need.

The creation of new materials also helped free people from the social and economic constraints imposed by the scarcity of natural resources. Inexpensive celluloid made material wealth more widespread and obtainable. And the plastics revolution was only getting started.

The Development of New Plastics

In 1907 Leo Baekeland invented Bakelite, the first fully synthetic plastic, meaning it contained no molecules found in nature. Baekeland had been searching for a synthetic substitute for shellac, a natural electrical insulator, to meet the needs of the rapidly electrifying United States. Bakelite was not only a good insulator; it was also durable, heat resistant, and, unlike celluloid, ideally suited for mechanical mass production. Marketed as "the material of a thousand uses," Bakelite could be shaped or molded into almost anything, providing endless possibilities.

Hyatt's and Baekeland's successes led major chemical companies to invest in the research and development of new polymers, and new plastics soon joined celluloid and Bakelite. While Hyatt and Baekeland had been searching for materials with specific properties, the new research programs sought new plastics for their own sake and worried about finding uses for them later.

Plastics Come of Age

World War II necessitated a great expansion of the plastics industry in the United States, as industrial might proved as important to victory as military success. The need to preserve scarce natural resources made the production of synthetic alternatives a priority. Plastics provided those substitutes. Nylon, invented by Wallace Carothers in 1935 as a synthetic silk, was used during the war for parachutes, ropes, body armor, helmet liners, and more. Plexiglas provided an alternative to glass for aircraft windows. A Time magazine article noted that because of the war, "plastics have been turned to new uses and the adaptability of plastics demonstrated all over again."[1] During World War II plastic production in the United States increased by 300%.

The surge in plastic production continued after the war ended. After experiencing the Great Depression and then World War II, Americans were ready to spend again, and much of what they bought was made of plastic. According to author Susan Freinkel, "In product after product, market after market, plastics challenged traditional materials and won, taking the place of steel in cars, paper and glass in packaging, and wood in furniture."[2] The possibilities of plastics gave some observers an almost utopian vision of a future with abundant material wealth thanks to an inexpensive, safe, sanitary substance that could be shaped by humans to their every whim.

Growing Concerns About Plastics

The unblemished optimism about plastics didn't last. In the postwar years there was a shift in American perceptions as plastics were no longer seen as unambiguously positive. Plastic debris in the oceans was first observed in the 1960s, a decade in which Americans became increasingly aware of environmental problems. Rachel Carson's 1962 book, Silent Spring, exposed the dangers of chemical pesticides. In 1969 a major oil spill occurred off the California coast and the polluted Cuyahoga River in Ohio caught fire, raising concerns about pollution. As awareness about environmental issues spread, the persistence of plastic waste began to trouble observers.

Plastic also gradually became a word used to describe that which was cheap, flimsy, or fake. In The Graduate, one of the top movies of 1968, Dustin Hoffman's character was urged by an older acquaintance to make a career in plastics. Audiences cringed along with Hoffman at what they saw as misplaced enthusiasm for an industry that, rather than being full of possibilities, was a symbol of cheap conformity and superficiality.

Plastic Problems: Waste and Health

Plastic's reputation fell further in the 1970s and 1980s as anxiety about waste increased. Plastic became a special target because, while so many plastic products are disposable, plastic lasts forever in the environment. It was the plastics industry that offered recycling as a solution. In the 1980s the plastics industry led an influential drive encouraging municipalities to collect and process recyclable materials as part of their waste-management systems. However, recycling is far from perfect, and most plastics still end up in landfills or in the environment. Grocery-store plastic bags have become a target for activists looking to ban one-use, disposable plastics, and several American cities have already passed bag bans. The ultimate symbol of the problem of plastic waste is the Great Pacific Garbage Patch, which has often been described as a swirl of plastic garbage the size of Texas floating in the Pacific Ocean.

The reputation of plastics has suffered further thanks to a growing concern about the potential threat they pose to human health. These concerns focus on the additives (such as the much-discussed bisphenol A [BPA] and a class of chemicals called phthalates) that go into plastics during the manufacturing process, making them more flexible, durable, and transparent. Some scientists and members of the public are concerned about evidence that these chemicals leach out of plastics and into our food, water, and bodies. In very high doses these chemicals can disrupt the endocrine (or hormonal) system. Researchers worry particularly about the effects of these chemicals on children and what continued accumulation means for future generations.

The Future of Plastics

Despite growing mistrust, plastics are critical to modern life. Plastics made possible the development of computers, cell phones, and most of the lifesaving advances of modern medicine. Lightweight and good for insulation, plastics help save fossil fuels used in heating and in transportation. Perhaps most important, inexpensive plastics raised the standard of living and made material abundance more readily available. Without plastics many possessions that we take for granted might be out of reach for all but the richest Americans. Replacing natural materials with plastic has made many of our possessions cheaper, lighter, safer, and stronger.

Since it's clear that plastics have a valuable place in our lives, some scientists are attempting to make plastics safer and more sustainable. Some innovators are developing bioplastics, which are made from plant crops instead of fossil fuels, to create substances that are more environmentally friendly than conventional plastics. Others are working to make plastics that are truly biodegradable. Some innovators are searching for ways to make recycling more efficient, and they even hope to perfect a process that converts plastics back into the fossil fuels from which they were derived. All of these innovators recognize that plastics are not perfect but that they are an important and necessary part of our future.

Endnotes

1. Joseph L. Nicholson and George R. Leighton, "Plastics Come of Age," Harper's Magazine, August 1942, p. 306.

2. Susan Freinkel, Plastics: A Toxic Love Story (New York: Henry Holt, 2011), p. 4.

Plastics and Disposability Are the Primary Problems with Consumption

Susan Strasser

Susan Strasser is an award-winning historian and a professor emerita of American History at the University of Delaware. She is the author of Satisfaction Guaranteed: The Making of the American Mass Market *and* Waste and Want: A Social History of Trash.

In 1957 Disneyland opened the Monsanto House of the Future, an all-plastic dwelling. Over the next 10 years millions of visitors passed through its fantastical rooms, designed by MIT architects with curved walls and large windows. The house was equipped with plastic chairs and plastic floors, the kitchen with precise stacks of plastic plates and plastic cups. Monsanto's house trumpeted the wonders of science, as well as the chemical industry and its products. Plastic, it proclaimed, was the material of tomorrow.

Tomorrow has come, and plastic is everywhere. In the half century since the Monsanto house closed, plastic has conquered the planet: globally, we now consume a million plastic bottles a minute and more than a trillion plastic bags every year.

Nobody lives in curved plastic rooms, but synthetic carpeting, vinyl flooring and laminate counters are all commonplace. And most Americans' daily routines depend on single-use items and throwaway plastic packaging, much of it flowing into streams and oceans, polluting our ecosystems. Tiny plastic fragments, off-gassing and effluents from plastic factories pollute our bodies. The plastic dream has become a plastic nightmare.

How did we get to this point? The history of plastic and of the very idea of disposability suggest that we and the planet have become victims of plastic's success. Synthetic materials took over our economy, our lifestyles, and our imaginations because they did their jobs so well.

Disposability

Disposability is not a new idea. Toilet paper was common by 1900; paper cups and paper towels were adopted as sanitary measures in public places during the following decades, though few were yet used in homes. Disposable razor blades and bottle caps came into common use around the same time.

But most Americans produced little trash, practicing habits of reuse that had prevailed in agricultural communities. They made soup from food scraps or fed them to animals; objects worthless to adults became playthings for children. People spent considerable time and effort taking care of things—oiling and waxing, mending and altering, working to prolong the useful lives of the things they owned.

By the 1920s, most families were moving toward a modern relationship to the material world. Convenience and cleanliness came to symbolize the goals of a modern lifestyle, a synonym for luxury, comfort and emancipation from worry and work.

Bakelite, the first plastic produced entirely from synthetic materials, was invented in 1907. By the beginning of the second world war, plastic was commonly accepted for industrial parts, automobile distributor caps and colorful costume jewelry. The chemical industry was widely celebrated for plastic's contributions to the war effort—nylon parachutes and ripcords, plastic airplane windshields, synthetic rubber wing linings. As soon as the war ended, major chemical companies pivoted from war production to consumer goods—DuPont, for instance, reconverted its factories to produce yarn for nylon stockings instead of parachutes.

People did not yet regard plastics as disposable. Indeed, most new synthetic materials were touted as indestructible. They replaced breakables such as ceramics and glass, and natural materials that deteriorated over time, such as wood, metal, cork and animal hides. Postwar construction incorporated durable new plastic floorings and countertops. In the kitchens and bathrooms of newly built suburbs, women tossed trash in plastic waste baskets and powdered their noses using plastic compacts.

Hyperbolic Language

By the 1960s, long-lasting plastics had been joined by plastic throwaways, including Saran Wrap, its more affordable competitors, and early plastic packaging. Shampoo came in glass bottles when I was a child in the 50s, but when plastic bottles came along we could stop washing our hair in fear of bloody feet in the shower.

Plastics were advertised in hyperbolic language. "Bottle magic," Dew deodorant crowed about its new squeeze bottle that "can't leak, break, or spill". LePage's liquid plastic glue offered "amazing strength and durability".

From the manufacturer's standpoint, the raw materials and fabrication processes were cheap and the finished goods lightweight. Consumers adopted synthetic materials gratefully because they were so effective. As Barry Commoner, one of the 20th century's greatest environmental thinkers, explained in his 1971 bestseller, The Closing Circle: "Plastics clutter the landscape because they are unnatural, synthetic substances designed to resist degradation—precisely the properties that are the basis of their technological value."

The new materials offered freedom from attention, care and responsibility for material things. They cut down on laundry, cleaning and dishwashing chores. A spotlessness and ease once attainable only with servants could now be achieved by buying things and by throwing things away.

Throwaway Culture

The transition to a throwaway consumer culture was complex and gradual: the young and the wealthy embraced new products first, while others lived as they always had. But eventually the shift was complete as people lost the knowledge of how to make things last, and the leftovers and scraps they might once have valued became trash instead.

Eventually an actual celebration of trashmaking emerged. As frozen foods were introduced during the 1950s, disposable packaging became an all-in-one problem solver: the Swanson brand frozen TV dinner and products from competitors like Banquet and Morton replaced pots, pans and plates, eliminating the need for dishwashing as well as cooking. At first, many consumers, unused to a throwaway lifestyle, washed them anyhow. My family amassed quite a collection of tins from frozen pot pies, the dinner of choice when my parents went out for the evening.

But soon more and more products were manufactured and sold with an understanding that they would soon be trash. Disposability rested on the ideas that somebody else would carry away the trash, that used materials were worthless, and that nobody need think about what happened to them.

Plastic became the basis for a new relationship to the material world: it required consumers to buy things rather than make them, to throw things out rather than fix them. Nobody made plastic at home, hardly anybody understood how it was made, it usually could not be repaired, and there was no way to return it to nature.

Single-Use Tsunami

On the first Earth Day in 1970, Americans were using nowhere near the level of plastics we now take for granted. The microwave oven had not yet taken off and frozen foods were still in foil, ketchup still came in glass bottles, and the shift from paper to plastic at the grocery store was more than a decade away. But the new materials spawned by the chemical industry had become normalized, and consumers generally appreciated and applauded them. The corporations that made consumer goods encouraged us to keep on buying, enriching those companies—as well as the chemical manufacturers, such as Monsanto, Dow and DuPont, and the fossil fuel industry.

Recent years have brought a tsunami of single-use plastics (straws, plastic bags, takeout containers, plastic water bottles). Nearly half the plastic ever produced has been manufactured since 2000. Even though many people alive today can remember a world without ubiquitous plastic, we still have a hard time remembering how we actually lived without it.

Even early on, the drawbacks were evident. In 1971, Commoner described the proliferation of plastic in the oceans—fragments of plastic ropes and nets. "These pollution problems arise not out of some minor inadequacies in the new technologies, but because of their very success in accomplishing their designed aims."

None of us live in exactly the future that the Monsanto House designers envisioned, but plastic has indeed become the defining material of our time. Recycling plastic turns out to be considerably more complex and technical than turning rags into paper or melting down metals. Producing plastic continues to create potential hazards that emerge as threats to public health. In exchange for indestructible, non-permeable solutions to everyday problems, as Commoner warned, "we have created for ourselves a new and dangerous world."

Sustainable Development Depends on Environmental, Social, and Economic Factors

Matthew Mason

Matthew Mason is a freelance education writer based in the UK whose writing focuses on environmental science. See his site at mgm-cs.com.

Sustainability is a broad discipline, giving students and graduates insights into most aspects of the human world from business to technology to environment and the social sciences. The core skills with which a graduates leaves college or university are highly sought after, especially in a modern world looking to drastically reduce carbon emissions and discover and develop the technologies of the future. Sustainability draws on politics, economics and, philosophy and other social sciences as well as the hard sciences. Sustainability skills and environmental awareness is a priority in many corporate jobs at graduate level and over as businesses seek to adhere to new legislation. Therefore, Sustainability graduates will go into many fields but most commonly civic planning, environmental consultancy (built and natural environment), agriculture, not for profit, corporate strategies, health assessment and planning, and even into law and decision making. Entry-level jobs are growing and over the coming years, bachelors graduates can expect more and more options and opportunities.

Sustainability is one the newest degree subjects that attempts to bridge social science with civic engineering and environmental science with the technology of the future. When we hear the word "sustainability" we tend to think of renewable fuel sources, reducing carbon emissions, protecting environments and a way of keeping the delicate ecosystems of our planet in balance. In short, sustainability looks to protect our natural environment, human and

"What Is Sustainability and Why Is It Important?" by Matthew Mason, EnvironmentalScience.org. Reprinted by permission.

ecological health, while driving innovation and not compromising our way of life. Because of this growing requirement, a master's will not necessarily be required for most jobs as bachelor's programs (and in some cases lower than this) prepares people for a career in sustainability.

What Is Sustainability?

The definition of "sustainability" is the study of how natural systems function, remain diverse and produce everything it needs for the ecology to remain in balance. It also acknowledges that human civilisation takes resources to sustain our modern way of life. There are countless examples throughout human history where a civilisation has damaged its own environment and seriously affected its own survival chances (some of which Jared Diamond explores in his book *Collapse: How Complex Societies Choose to Fail or Survive*). Sustainability takes into account how we might live in harmony with the natural world around us, protecting it from damage and destruction.

We now live in a modern, consumerist and largely urban existence throughout the developed world and we consume a lot of natural resources every day. In our urban centres, we consume more power than those who live in rural settings and urban centres use a lot more power than average, keeping our streets and civic buildings lit, to power our appliances, our heating and other public and household power requirements. That's not to say that sustainable living should only focus on people who live in urban centres though, there are improvements to be made everywhere— it is estimated that we use about 40% more resources every year than we can put back and that needs to change. Sustainability and sustainable development focuses on balancing that fine line between competing needs—our need to move forward technologically and economically, and the needs to protect the environments in which we and others live. Sustainability is not just about the environment, it's also about our health as a society in ensuring that no people or areas of life suffer as a result of environmental legislation, and it's also about examining the longer term effects of the actions humanity takes and asking questions about how it may be improved.

The Three Pillars of Sustainability

In 2005, the World Summit on Social Development identified three core areas that contribute to the philosophy and social science of sustainable development. These "pillars" in many national standards and certification schemes, form the backbone of tackling the core areas that the world now faces. The Brundtland Commission described it as "development that meets the needs of the present without compromising the ability of future generations to meet their own needs". We must consider the future then, in making our decisions about the present.

Economic Development

This is the issue that proves the most problematic as most people disagree on political ideology what is and is not economically sound, and how it will affect businesses and by extension, jobs and employability. It is also about providing incentives for businesses and other organisations to adhere to sustainability guidelines beyond their normal legislative requirements. Also, to encourage and foster incentives for the average person to do their bit where and when they can; one person can rarely achieve much, but taken as a group, effects in some areas are cumulative. The supply and demand market is consumerist in nature and modern life requires a lot of resources every single day; for the sake of the environment, getting what we consume under control is the paramount issue. Economic development is about giving people what they want without compromising quality of life, especially in the developing world, and reducing the financial burden and "red tape" of doing the right thing.

Social Development

There are many facets to this pillar. Most importantly is awareness of and legislation protection of the health of people from pollution and other harmful activities of business and other organisations. In North America, Europe and the rest of the developed world, there are strong checks and programmes of legislation in place to ensure that people's health and wellness is strongly protected. It is also about maintaining access to basic resources without compromising the quality of life. The biggest hot topic for many people right now is sustainable housing and how we can better build the homes we live in from sustainable material. The final element is education— encouraging people to participate in environmental sustainability and teaching them about the effects of environmental protection as well as warning of the dangers if we cannot achieve our goals.

Environmental Protection

We all know what we need to do to protect the environment, whether that is recycling, reducing our power consumption by switching electronic devices off rather than using standby, by walking short journeys instead of taking the bus. Businesses are regulated to prevent pollution and to keep their own carbon emissions low. There are incentives to installing renewable power sources in our homes and businesses. Environmental protection is the third pillar and to many, the primary concern of the future of humanity. It defines how we should study and protect ecosystems, air quality, integrity and sustainability of our resources and focusing on the elements that place stress on the environment. It also concerns how technology will drive our greener future; the EPA recognized that developing technology and biotechnology is key to this sustainability, and protecting the environment of the future from potential damage that technological advances could potentially bring.

What Are the Primary Goals of Sustainability?

The sustainable development professional network thinks, acts and works globally. In 2012, the United Nations Conference on Sustainable Development met to discuss and develop a set of goals to work towards; they grew out of the Millennium Development Goals (MDG) that claimed success in reducing global poverty while acknowledging there was still much more to do. The SDG eventually came up with a list of 17 items which included amongst other things:

- The end of poverty and hunger
- Better standards of education and healthcare—particularly as it pertains to water quality and better sanitation
- To achieve gender equality
- Sustainable economic growth while promoting jobs and stronger economies
- All of the above and more while tackling the effects of climate change, pollution and other environmental factors that can harm and do harm people's health, livelihoods and lives.
- Sustainability to include health of the land, air and sea

Finally, it acknowledged the concept of nature having certain rights—that people have stewardship of the world and the importance of putting people at the forefront of solving the above global issues through management of the environment and of consumption (for example, reducing packaging and discouraging food waste as well as promoting the use of recyclable materials).

History of Sustainability

Humans have, since the Neolithic Agricultural Revolution and maybe even before then, been a consumer rather than a replenisher of environmental resources. From hunter-gatherer societies that moved into an area to use up its resources in a season before setting up camp or moving on, only to return the following year to do the same, the development of a surplus economy saw permanent settlements. Slash and burn farming replaced natural wilderness often with uniform crop plantation and camps gave way to settlements, then eventually villages, towns and cities which would put pressure on the environment.

Sometimes, the environmental pressures forced people into making these changes in the first place (growing human population being one of those pressures) and often eventually they had to move on to somewhere new where the environmental could better sustain them and their practices, or make further changes to their existing environment. There was no real concept of sustainable living, even if the people of the distant past understood that soil had a maximum fertility that could be exhausted and replenished with livestock.

It is widely acknowledged that many societies collapsed due to an inability to adapt to the conditions brought on by these unsustainable practices. Whether that was introducing alien species that upset the balance of the ecosystem, cutting down too many trees at once or even a failure to adapt to natural fluctuations in the climate, we are far more aware in the modern world about the potential damage caused by human action. Cultural change often led to survival of those societies beyond what might have been expected under the circumstances.

Though some Renaissance and Enlightenment philosophers would express concern about resources and over-population and whether these were sustainable in the long term, these people were not taken seriously at the time other than as a hypothetical question. It would take until the 20th century before we would understand the impact that we could have on our environment. Environmental damage, pollution, destabilising soils by cutting down trees, fossil fuels and other environmental issues led to a growing concern about the environment and whether we were or could damage our own ecosystem. The United Nations was founded after World War II and in 1945, UNESCO was established to promote the importance of human culture and of science. Today, their remit is "to contribute to the building of peace, the eradication of poverty, sustainable development and intercultural dialogue through education, the sciences, culture, communication and information".

By the late 20th century, the science of climate change was firmly established. We knew by the 1980s about the problems of the greenhouse effect and the destruction of the ozone layer and coming very late in the century, an awareness of the notion that some of our resources—particularly fossil fuels—were finite and that we should make efforts to move to renewable methods of power. It was then that we saw the social, economic and scientific birth of the environmental movement.

A Sustainable Future

It is not yet clear what our sustainable future will look like but with emerging technologies and the improvement of older cleaner fuel sources, many people now look to a post fossil fuel world—including businesses. Since the 1950s, we have experienced unprecedented growth including intensive farming, a technological revolution and a massive increase in our power needs putting even greater pressure and strain on the planet's resources. We are also far more aware of the plight of the developing world and that facing our planet as we now observe both natural and human-caused disasters and the effects that these can have on the ecosystems and on human population. It's vital that we develop new, cleaner technologies to cope with our energy demands but sustainability is not just about the environment.

The biggest social activism movement related to the social development side of sustainability, has been programs such as Fair Trade and the Rainforest Alliance in encouraging good farming practices while ensuring farmers who produce luxury goods such as coffee and cocoa receive a decent living wage. Activist and sustainability professionals hope to remove trade barriers in future so that they may benefit everyone, contributing to the economic and social development core of sustainability while promoting good environmental practice.

Manufacturing Is Becoming More Sustainable

Joseph Rauch

Joseph Rauch worked as a content marketing specialist at Thomas Publishing. He is now a content marketing manager at Public Goods.

For more than a decade, "sustainability" has been one of those vague buzzwords that has meandered in and out of the spotlight of our collective vocabulary. Some people look for the term when they shop online or browse the aisles of their grocery stores. Many brands have marketed environmentally-friendly products to consumers who value the sense of positively contributing to their ecosystems, of feeling like they are part of a solution.

It is true that sustainability, in any context, ultimately relates to human impact on the environment. For manufacturers, however, the term has a much more detailed definition:

> Sustainable manufacturing is the creation of manufactured products through economically-sound processes that minimize negative environmental impacts while conserving energy and natural resources. Sustainable manufacturing also enhances employee, community and product safety.

In the industrial space, sustainability is primarily a business practice that considers the people who are making the products, in addition to the customers and the world they live in. Reducing harmful emissions can be both a direct goal and an indirect result of efficient manufacturing.

There are many types of sustainable industrial strategies that allow companies to save money, be environmentally responsible, remain competitive, and develop an attractive workplace culture. By examining every form of sustainability, manufacturers can fully understand the idea and decide how much they want to invest in the practice.

"How Sustainable Practices Are Changing the Manufacturing Sphere," by Joseph Rauch, ThomasNet.com, June 19, 2018. Reprinted by permission.

Efficient and Cost-Effective Manufacturing Processes That Reduce Waste

Because the Environmental Protection Agency [EPA] knows cost-effective manufacturing can ultimately diminish effects that are detrimental to local ecosystems, the organization has a history of rewarding efficient industrial businesses. In 2006 the agency acknowledged Canyon Creek Cabinet Company for "lean manufacturing."

By reducing lead time and material waste, in one year the company saved roughly a million dollars and increased cabinet production from 900 per day to about 1,000. This accomplishment resulted in less hazardous byproducts and energy consumption.

Ryan Chan, founder of work order software company UpKeep, stated that companies can use sustainable practices to address at least seven sources of waste:

1. Defects
2. Motion
3. Transportation
4. Inventory
5. Extra processing
6. Waiting
7. Overproduction

Recyclable and Sustainable Materials

Many companies incorporate sustainability into production itself, not only the efficiency of their processes. Athyron, for example, is a Texas-based manufacturer that uses recycled materials to produce Miura, an alternative to wood. The company's sources include agricultural byproducts such as rice and peanut hulls, as well as plastic waste and nylon from recycled carpets.

Miura is not only a method of conserving trees and forests. The substance has advantages over wood, such as being immune to termites and rotting.

Sustainable manufacturing materials can also provide a competitive advantage in fields plagued with pollution problems. In the nanomaterial sector, a source for everything from dental implants to food packaging, there are regulations that restrict certain classes of chemicals because of their toxicity.

These policies paved a market penetration route for Boco Technologies, a company that produces sustainable nanomaterials from crustacean shells. Director Aaron Guan said this shift has improved customer perception of the industry.

Optimized Business Operations and Facilities

Every manufacturer utilizes at least one facility to create their products, participate in the supply chain process, and provide office space for employees. Because of basic necessities such as temperature control, lighting, gas, plumbing, water and electricity to power machines, simply running the business has an impact on the environment. Industrial companies can save money and resources by optimizing their operations.

For example, in 2009 a ThyssenKrupp elevators plant in Waupaca Wisconsin received a state environmental award for installing a system that recovered and recirculated heat that otherwise would have escaped and been wasted. This structure fueled heat during winter and supplied hot water to the facility, all at a lower cost.

Eco-conscious Shipping Practices

The vast majority of shipping vehicles consume natural resources and emit exhaust. When they do not need to travel as far, the people involved in this aspect of the supply chain process usually save both time and money. There is less pollution and more fuel remaining for other trips.

Manufacturers can participate in sustainable shipping by collaborating with nearby suppliers and companies. This dynamic also contributes to local economies that are often in desperate need of stimulation.

Sustainable Packaging

Boxes are relatively easy to recycle, but not all packing materials have that quality. Manufacturers need to be mindful of how they are packaging parts and products. This attitude can be cost-effective and sustainable.

Southern Designs, a company that offers laser cutting — among other services — for industrial clients, invested in a corrugated packaging machine that produces boxes on demand with customizable sizes. This practice has reduced the need for void filling supplies such as paper, air pillows and bubble wrap, according to Founder Tance Hughes.

Fortunately Southern Designs is one of many businesses that has invested in sustainable packaging. Supplier demand for sustainable packaging recently spiked, according to a Thomas Index Report. Large enterprises such as Amazon and Coca-Cola have pledged to make 100% of their packaging sustainable in the coming decade.

Basic Recycling

This may seem like a simple and obvious issue, but lot of companies do not recycle properly. Only 34% of recyclable materials are processed sustainably, according to an EPA report. Manufacturers can help by to recycling as many materials as possible, and to do so in a way that is congruent with other aspects of sustainability.

Consumer Safety and Health

Perhaps the most important role manufacturers can play is ensuring their products and services are not dangerous or harmful to the health of consumers. To that end, manufacturers should be investing in excellent quality assurance. At least a few employees should be dedicated to this tenet, and every company should consider investing in an enterprise resource planning system [ERP] that will provide accountability. Manufacturers also need to adhere to laws and regulations regarding consumer safety and health.

This issue relates to the use of sustainable materials. There is an EPA-approved antimicrobial copper alloy, for example, that constantly fights bacteria.

Employee Safety and Health

Unfortunately, employers often overlook or neglect this crucial tenet. People who work on the floor in manufacturing plants and facilities are sometimes exposed to hazardous or dangerous situations. Companies have an obligation to care for their workers by meeting industry health standards.

This concern includes mental health as well. To foster a healthy environment, leaders and managers should treat their subordinates with respect and courtesy. Working hours and shift times should be reasonable as well, allowing employees to refresh and work at their best.

Every Facet of Manufacturing Sustainability is Connected

Adopting sustainable manufacturing practices can result in cost savings, efficiency improvements, and a better workplace. While the process may seem daunting, the payoff is definitely worth it.

Consuming Less Would Create a More Fulfilling Way of Life

Samuel Alexander

Samuel Alexander is a research fellow at the Melbourne Sustainable Society Institute of the University of Melbourne, where he is also a lecturer with the Office for Environmental Programs. He is the co-author of Degrowth in the Suburbs: A Radical Urban Imaginary and Carbon Civilisation and the Energy Descent Future.

What does genuine economic progress look like? The orthodox answer is that a bigger economy is always better, but this idea is increasingly strained by the knowledge that, on a finite planet, the economy can't grow for ever.

This week's Addicted to Growth conference in Sydney is exploring how to move beyond growth economics and towards a "steady-state" economy.

But what is a steady-state economy? Why it is it desirable or necessary? And what would it be like to live in?

The Global Predicament

We used to live on a planet that was relatively empty of humans; today it is full to overflowing, with more people consuming more resources. We would need one and a half Earths to sustain the existing economy into the future. Every year this ecological overshoot continues, the foundations of our existence, and that of other species, are undermined.

At the same time, there are great multitudes around the world who are, by any humane standard, under-consuming, and the humanitarian challenge of eliminating global poverty is likely to increase the burden on ecosystems still further.

Meanwhile the population is set to hit 11 billion this century. Despite this, the richest nations still seek to grow their economies without apparent limit.

Like a snake eating its own tail, our growth-orientated civilisation suffers from the delusion that there are no environmental limits to growth. But rethinking growth in an age of limits cannot be avoided. The only question is whether it will be by design or disaster.

Degrowth to a Steady-State Economy

The idea of the steady-state economy presents us with an alternative. This term is somewhat misleading, however, because it suggests that we simply need to maintain the size of the existing economy and stop seeking further growth.

But given the extent of ecological overshoot—and bearing in mind that the poorest nations still need some room to develop their economies and allow the poorest billions to attain a dignified level of existence—the transition will require the richest nations to downscale radically their resource and energy demands.

This realisation has given rise to calls for economic "degrowth". To be distinguished from recession, degrowth means a phase of planned and equitable economic contraction in the richest nations, eventually reaching a steady state that operates within Earth's biophysical limits.

At this point, mainstream economists will accuse degrowth advocates of misunderstanding the potential of technology, markets, and efficiency gains to "decouple" economic growth from environmental impact. But there is no misunderstanding here. Everyone knows that we could produce and consume more efficiently than we do today. The problem is that efficiency without sufficiency is lost.

Despite decades of extraordinary technological advancement and huge efficiency improvements, the energy and resource demands of the global economy are still increasing. This is because within a growth-orientated economy, efficiency gains tend to be reinvested in more consumption and more growth, rather than in reducing impact.

This is the defining, critical flaw in growth economics: the false assumption that all economies across the globe can continue growing while radically reducing environmental impact to a sustainable level. The extent of decoupling required is simply too great. As we try unsuccessfully to "green" capitalism, we see the face of Gaia vanishing.

The very lifestyles that were once considered the definition of success are now proving to be our greatest failure. Attempting to universalise affluence would be catastrophic. There is absolutely no way that today's 7.2 billion people could live the Western way of life, let alone the 11 billion expected in the future. Genuine progress now lies beyond growth. Tinkering around the edges of capitalism will not cut it.

We need an alternative.

Enough for Everyone, Forever

When one first hears calls for degrowth, it is easy to think that this new economic vision must be about hardship and deprivation; that it means going back to the stone age, resigning ourselves to a stagnant culture, or being anti-progress. Not so.

Degrowth would liberate us from the burden of pursuing material excess. We simply don't need so much stuff—certainly not if it comes at the cost of planetary health, social justice, and personal well-being. Consumerism is a gross failure of imagination, a debilitating addiction that degrades nature and doesn't even satisfy the universal human craving for meaning.

Degrowth, by contrast, would involve embracing what has been termed the "simpler way"—producing and consuming less.

This would be a way of life based on modest material and energy needs but nevertheless rich in other dimensions—a life of frugal abundance. It is about creating an economy based on sufficiency, knowing how much is enough to live well, and discovering that enough is plenty.

The lifestyle implications of degrowth and sufficiency are far more radical than the "light green" forms of sustainable consumption that are widely discussed today. Turning off the lights, taking shorter showers, and recycling are all necessary parts of what sustainability will require of us, but these measures are far from enough.

But this does not mean we must live a life of painful sacrifice. Most of our basic needs can be met in quite simple and low-impact ways, while maintaining a high quality of life.

What Would Life Be Like in a Degrowth Society?

In a degrowth society we would aspire to localise our economies as far and as appropriately as possible. This would assist with reducing carbon-intensive global trade, while also building resilience in the face of an uncertain and turbulent future.

Through forms of direct or participatory democracy we would organise our economies to ensure that everyone's basic needs are met, and then redirect our energies away from economic expansion. This would be a relatively low-energy mode of living that ran primarily on renewable energy systems.

Renewable energy cannot sustain an energy-intensive global society of high-end consumers. A degrowth society embraces the necessity of "energy descent", turning our energy crises into an opportunity for civilisational renewal.

We would tend to reduce our working hours in the formal economy in exchange for more home-production and leisure. We would have less income, but more freedom. Thus, in our simplicity, we would be rich.

Wherever possible, we would grow our own organic food, water our gardens with water tanks, and turn our neighbourhoods into edible landscapes as the Cubans have done in Havana. As my friend Adam Grubb so delightfully declares, we should "eat the suburbs", while supplementing urban agriculture with food from local farmers' markets.

We do not need to purchase so many new clothes. Let us mend or exchange the clothes we have, buy second-hand, or make our own. In a degrowth society, the fashion and marketing industries would quickly wither away. A new aesthetic of sufficiency would develop, where we creatively re-use and refashion the vast existing stock of clothing and materials, and explore less impactful ways of producing new clothes.

We would become radical recyclers and do-it-yourself experts. This would partly be driven by the fact that we would simply be living in an era of relative scarcity, with reduced discretionary income.

But human beings find creative projects fulfilling, and the challenge of building the new world within the shell of the old promises to be immensely meaningful, even if it will also entail times of trial. The apparent scarcity of goods can also be greatly reduced by scaling up the sharing economy, which would also enrich our communities.

One day, we might even live in cob houses that we build ourselves, but over the next few critical decades the fact is that most of us will be living within the poorly designed urban infrastructure that already exists. We are hardly going to knock it all down and start again. Instead, we must 'retrofit the suburbs', as leading permaculturalist David Holmgren argues. This would involve doing everything we can to make our homes more energy-efficient, more productive, and probably more densely inhabited.

This is not the eco-future that we are shown in glossy design magazines featuring million-dollar "green homes" that are prohibitively expensive.

Degrowth offers a more humble—and I would say more realistic—vision of a sustainable future.

Making the Change

A degrowth transition to a steady-state economy could happen in a variety of ways. But the nature of this alternative vision suggests that the changes will need to be driven from the "bottom up", rather than imposed from the "top down".

What I have written above highlights a few of the personal and household aspects of a degrowth society based on sufficiency (for much more detail, see here and here). Meanwhile, the 'transition towns' movement shows how whole communities can engage with the idea.

But it is critical to acknowledge the social and structural constraints that currently make it much more difficult than it needs to be to adopt a lifestyle of sustainable consumption. For example, it is hard to drive less in the absence of safe bike lanes and good public transport; it is hard find a work-life balance if access to basic housing burdens us with excessive debt; and it is hard to re-imagine the good life if we are constantly bombarded with advertisements insisting that "nice stuff" is the key to happiness.

Actions at the personal and household levels will never be enough, on their own, to achieve a steady-state economy. We need to create new, post-capitalist structures and systems that promote, rather than inhibit, the simpler way of life. These wider changes will never emerge, however, until we have a culture that demands them. So first and foremost, the revolution that is needed is a revolution in consciousness.

I do not present these ideas under the illusion that they will be readily accepted. The ideology of growth clearly has a firm grip on our society and beyond. Rather, I hold up degrowth up as the most coherent framework for understanding the global predicament and signifying the only desirable way out of it.

The alternative is to consume ourselves to death under the false banner of "green growth", which would not be smart economics.

Economic Growth Stands in the Way of Sustainability

Juliette Legendre

Juliette Legendre is a research associate with the State Fiscal Project team of the Center on Budget and Policy Priorities. Her research focuses on immigration and climate policies.

G rowth is the "beating heart of a free economy," U.S. House Speaker Paul Ryan told the Economic Club of Washington D.C, earlier this year. In his speech, Ryan repeated the common narrative that without steady economic growth, we're all doomed.

Degrowthers—members of a flourishing movement of academics and activists pushing to equitably and sustainably downscale the economy—think otherwise.

Growth is not a solution, but a part of the problem, degrowthers argue, and cannot be endless in a world with finite resources. It perpetuates a cycle of consumption and production, putting the planet and our well-being at great risk. But, despite all the costs, economic growth continues to be the raison d'etre in politics and the business sector.

The GDP, or Gross Domestic Product, measures the value added of goods and services produced in a country during a given period. It's widely considered the king of all popular indicators for tracking economic growth, often used to score political points. U.S. President Donald Trump cheered the 4.1 percent GDP growth in the second quarter of 2018—the highest rate since 2014—calling it "amazing" during an impromptu press conference in July.

But what Trump failed to mention is that a bigger economic pie does not necessarily translate into higher living standards for everyone. That's especially true in a deeply unequal society

"The Degrowth Movement Challenges the Conventional Wisdom on Economic Health," by Juliette Legendre, Inequality, September 3, 2018. https://inequality.org/great-divide/degrowth-movement-economic-health/. Licensed under CC BY 3.0.

like the United States, where the benefits of economic growth are increasingly captured by the 1 percent.

In an interview with The Washington Post, David Pilling, the journalist and author of The Growth Delusion: Wealth, Poverty, and the Well-Being of Nations, says GDP measures economic "quantity not quality" and should not be conflated with well-being, especially in richer countries. In some instances, GDP growth could even mean the opposite.

GDP has long been widely criticized for counting defense spending, financial speculation, and even theft as positive contributions to growth, while excluding non-monetized trade and ignoring environmental and social costs. "If I steal your car and sell it, that counts toward growth," Pilling explains, "but if I look after an aged relative or bring up three well-adjusted children, that does not."

Pilling recommends complementing GDP with more inclusive data and measurements. But the leaders of the degrowth movement don't just challenge growth indicators. They're taking on the dogma of economic growth.

Degrowth "does not call for doing less of the same," as the editors of the first comprehensive book on the movement make clear. "The objective is not to make an elephant leaner, but to turn an elephant into a snail." They call for a radically different political-economic system needed to preserve the environment and improve well-being.

The term décroissance—French for degrowth—was first used decades ago by European intellectuals. But the term became the umbrella slogan for a movement in 2008, when an academic collective organized the first international degrowth conference in Paris.

Conference-goers made the term concrete, defining degrowth as a "voluntary transition towards a just, participatory, and ecologically sustainable society," making clear that a downsizing process was necessary for wealthy countries. They envisioned a society organized around sharing, simplicity, and solidarity, rather than the profit, efficiency, and competition inherent to capitalism.

In the decade since the Paris conference, six other international gatherings have further cemented their ideas, including at this year's meeting in Sweden. These conferences have helped shape an international degrowth community of academics, activists and practitioners.

The movement is also solidifying the global nature of its message. The first North-South degrowth conference is being held this week in Mexico City. The gathering is crucial: a frequent criticism of the degrowth movement is that the economies of Global South countries have the same right to grow to meet basic needs that Northern countries have. Sociologist Miriam Lang responded to this criticism at the Malmö conference. The economic "growth" that critics point to as being necessary, Lang said, generally rely on natural resource extraction and other industries that exploit local populations, reinforcing a destructive ideal of progress.

The degrowth movement is more of a coalition of social and environmental ideas rather than one cohesive force with a unified political agenda. One shared understanding, however, is the need for systemic change. The next step for degrowthers? Developing a plan for a radical transformation.

A survey of published scholarship on degrowth found that policy proposals align with three broad goals:

- Reduce the environmental impact of human activities
- Redistribute income and wealth both within and between countries;
- Promote the transition from a materialistic to a convivial and participatory society.

The proposals include common-sense ecological plans, like the reduction of energy and material consumption, carbon caps, bans on harmful activities, and incentives for local production and consumption. Degrowthers are also looking to transform traditional ideas of the economy with the promotion of community currencies and alternative credit institutions, reduced working hours, basic and maximum incomes, and voluntary simplicity and downshifting.

These proposals are gaining traction in the political sphere. In the UK, economist Tim Jackson has promoted an all-party working group in the UK Parliament devoted to discussion and research on limiting growth. Jackson will also be a keynote speaker later this month at the European Parliament's Post-Growth 2018 conference. The gathering offers activists and scientists a unique opportunity to directly engage with EU officials on degrowth, and to present alternative to the dominant economic and financial orthodoxy.

The conference couldn't be more necessary, as European politicians are already coming up against the limits of growth. French environmental minister Nicolas Hulot resigned last week, frustrated at the lack of support he received to tackle urgent environmental issues while Macron and his government "stubbornly try to revive an economic model that is the cause of all this mess." Hulot is ringing an alarm that's all too familiar to degrowthers: we can't deal with our environmental crises without radically rethinking the economy.

Consume Less to Protect the Planet's Finite Resources

Sophie Perryer

Sophie Perryer is an editor at Factal News *and a freelance writer who has been published by* the Independent, World Finance, *and other publications. She is based in London.*

In every sphere of our commercialised, consumerist world, growth and success are seemingly inseparable. From national economic expansion to personal development, growth has become a proxy for obtaining health and wealth through constantly striving for bigger, better and more.

Yet, according to proponents of the degrowth movement, our environments can only support this consistent upward trajectory for so long. 'Degrowthers' argue that, on a planet of finite resources, endless growth is impossible and harms not only the world around us, but also our wellbeing. Instead, they advocate a transition away from growth and towards a more equitable and sustainable society that fulfils all of its economic actors.

The radical nature of degrowth principles has historically inhibited their spread outside of left-leaning academic circles. In recent years, however, with environmental issues becoming increasingly difficult to ignore and confidence in traditional economic markers such as GDP declining, the movement is gathering pace.

Sustainability's Sister

The term 'degrowth' was first proposed in the 1970s by the Franco-Austrian philosopher André Gorz, but it did not emerge as a movement until the late 2000s, when the first international degrowth conferences were held in Paris and Barcelona in 2008 and

"Cutting Back: How the Degrowth Movement Could Save the Planet," by Sophie Perryer and first appeared in European CEO Magazine, October 7, 2019. Reprinted by permission.

2010 respectively. "These were landmark events that cast this radical movement onto the global stage," Brendan Gleeson, Director of the Melbourne Sustainable Society Institute, told European CEO.

Some of the ideas associated with the degrowth movement have since entered mainstream socioeconomic debate, particularly in connection with sustainability. For example, Sara Fromm, a sustainability activist and member of Research & Degrowth, has noticed the term being used by the Spanish media in reference to mass tourism in Barcelona. "[Their reporting] probably doesn't cover everything that the degrowth movement wants to express with this term, but it still encompasses a lot of the values that those in the movement want to touch upon, particularly in terms of aviation," she said.

The degrowth and sustainability movements certainly share common ground, particularly with regards to reducing consumption. Taking fewer flights, eschewing fast fashion, purchasing less packaged food and committing to growing produce at home are all examples of mutual initiatives. Degrowthers, however, recognise that these individual changes, while valuable in contributing to wider environmental goals, will not achieve the sort of systemic change that they believe is necessary.

"Most sustainability advocates, including policymakers in government, still seem locked into the growth paradigm, holding on to hope that technological advances and green policy will be able to achieve sustainability without transcending the growth paradigm," said Gleeson. "Degrowth does not accept that techno-optimistic faith."

Less Is More

The degrowth movement pushes for a total redefinition of the way we live, centred on the rejection of expansionist economics. This extends beyond lifestyle and into political activism, along with a radical shift in working culture. Degrowthers argue that to transition away from growth we must reduce our working hours and dedicate more time to voluntary, community-led activities that promote fulfilment through non-consumptive means. "This does not mean committing to an impoverished life, but rather to finding joy and pleasure and satisfaction in new non-consumerist ways," said Gleeson.

This is something that Fromm has grappled with since engaging with the degrowth movement. She is currently a part-time consultant on sustainable projects, but dedicates the rest of her working week to voluntary work, spending time with family and advocating for the degrowth cause. However, she has found that her decision to eschew the traditional working week raised eyebrows among her peers. "I have certainly experienced people being confused about the choices I made because they have a different understanding of how to live your life and how much money you need to [sustain that]," she said.

Fromm believes that part of this scepticism can be attributed to social attitudes surrounding part-time work. "From my perspective, when it comes to enterprises, it is still not a very common thing," she said. "[Part-time workers] can be regarded as possibly a bit less important, not in leading positions, or oftentimes women that are caring for children. I would like to see it become accepted and implemented not only for those people but for anyone [who] has decided, for any reason, that they don't want to spend as much time on paid labour."

All or Nothing

Changing people's perceptions of work, however, is just one hurdle to overcome: there's also the financial aspect, which, in an inflationary society, presents a greater challenge. Degrowth theorists present two solutions to this issue: first, they suggest heavily investing in basic services such as healthcare and education to close the chasm that lower incomes will create. They argue that this would also help tackle social inequality by ensuring everyone has access to the same care and support.

The second, more controversial, proposed solution is the provision of a universal basic income (UBI), paid by the state to every citizen over the age of 18. "This would allow people to do more work within their communities and be among friends and family," said Fromm. The concept is not a new one, but it has gained traction in recent years and has been trialled in Canada, Uganda, Kenya and, most recently, Finland.

During the two-year Finnish programme, participants were given €560 per month, no strings attached. While UBI was not found to affect the participants' ability to find work, it did have a positive impact on the health, stress and concentration levels of those receiving it compared with those in the control group. "Those in the test group were also considerably more confident in their own future and their ability to influence societal issues," noted the researchers who carried out the study.

The wellness-boosting aspect of UBI certainly fits in with the degrowth movement's overall ethos of turning away from expansion in favour of more holistic markers of success. Paradoxically, the fact that the UBI did not have an impact on the participants' ability to find work also supports the argument that individual degrowth policies will not prove successful on their own. Introducing a UBI in a society that is still geared towards growth will not work as the two are fundamentally at odds with one another. For the UBI to bear fruit, it must form part of a systemic shift.

The all-or-nothing nature of the degrowth movement makes it somewhat intimidating, but Gleeson argues that the first and most important step is persuading people that a non-materialistic life is a more fulfilling one. "Consumer culture promises people that the path to happiness lies in increasing material wealth… but this is just a flawed conception of the good life," he said. "We need to structure our societies to ensure that everyone has enough, but our systems and cultures should then redirect energy away from materialistic pursuits and promote the good life through non-materialistic sources of meaning and happiness. In short, less (but enough) stuff, but more time and freedom."

Radical Action

This culture change is already underway in some countries. In May this year, New Zealand Prime Minister Jacinda Ardern announced a new 'wellbeing budget' for the country, with billions in new funding allocated to mental health services and measures to reduce child poverty.

Ardern said at the time: "We're embedding that notion of making decisions that aren't just about growth for growth's sake, but how are our people faring? How is our environment doing? These are the measures that will give us a true measure of our success." Bhutan has taken this philosophy further still by adopting 'gross national happiness' instead of GDP as the ultimate social goal. "It's arguably an example of a post-growth society," said Gleeson.

Unquestionably, degrowth is a radical philosophy – but we live in a time that requires radical action. Every environmental marker points to the fact that our world as we know it will not exist in 50 years if we continue at the current rate of resource consumption. "Ultimately, an economics of sufficiency is needed if we are going to live within the sustainable carrying capacity of the planet," Gleeson concluded. "There is no alternative."

Drastic Action Is Needed to Reduce the Impacts of Climate Change

United Nations Development Programme

The United Nations Development Programme (UNDP) is the UN's global development network, which works with countries and territories around the world to eradicate poverty, reduce inequality, and encourage investment and cooperation between countries.

The world needs to redouble its efforts to reach the Sustainable Development Goals, according to a United Nations Sustainable Development Goals (SDGs) Report launched today.

Released on the first day of the High-Level Political Forum taking place in New York from 9 to 18 July, the report raises the red flag that despite the achievements made, the world must adjust the pace and path of current efforts.

"While we are making notable progress to achieve all 17 SDGs by the year 2030, the Sustainable Development Goals Report released today clearly highlights that we still face a number of diverse challenges to accelerate the achievement of the Goals," said Achim Steiner, the Administrator of the United Nations Development Programme (UNDP). "The targets that countries have set themselves are ambitious and are wide-ranging—they include poverty reduction; the sweeping actions that we need to take to tackle climate change; as well as the increased efforts that are needed to protect our planet's biodiversity."

Report findings show that the rate of extreme poverty is falling, down to 8.6 per cent in 2018 from 36 per cent in 1990. However, the speed of poverty reduction is stalling. Gender inequality is also persistent as women and girls continue to be excluded from politics, education, and economic opportunities.

"The World Must Go Faster and Farther to Achieve the Sustainable Development Goals, New Report Says," United Nations Development Programme, July 9, 2019. Reprinted by permission.

Drastic action is needed to mitigate the climate change reality. The Paris Agreement is one step, with countries outlining their national contributions to cutting greenhouse gasses. The report shows that 2018 was the warmest year on record, while levels of carbon dioxide continue to rise, setting off a chain reaction of ocean acidification, more frequent extreme weather and sea level rises, among other symptoms.

The report also highlights encouraging news. The world is making headway on access to energy and the report shows that nearly nine out of 10 people have access to electricity, of which renewable technologies are playing an increasingly positive role.

Overall biodiversity loss is slowing, yet still fragile. The pace of deforestation has slowed by 25 per cent while funding for forest protection and management has increased. However, we must be diligent to prevent the extinction of one million species at risk, and halt any further land degradation.

As co-chair of the Task Team for the High-level Political Forum with the Department of Economic and Social Affairs, UNDP assisted in researching and writing this report.

The findings of the report will be explored further at the SDG Summit in September 2019, where Heads of State will gather to fully assess progress and ways to accelerate progress on the Goals.

This Summit will be the first of its kind since the 2015 adoption of the SDGs.

Organizations to Contact

The editors have compiled the following list of organizations concerned with the issues debated in this book. The descriptions are derived from materials provided by the organizations. All have publications or information available for interested readers. This list was compiled on the date of publication of the present volume; the information provided here may change. Be aware that many organizations take several weeks or longer to respond to inquiries, so allow as much time as possible.

Environmental Defense Fund (EDF)
1875 Connecticut Ave., NW, Suite 600, Washington, DC 20009
phone: (202) 572-3298
website: www.edf.org

The Environmental Defense Fund is a nonprofit environmental advocacy organization that was founded in 1967 and is based in the United States. It advocates for market-based solutions to environmental issues. It promotes the use of science, economics, and law to find nonpartisan solutions and works with scientists and policy experts from around the world.

Environmental Protection Agency (EPA)
1200 Pennsylvania Avenue, NW, Washington, DC 20460
phone: (202) 564-4700
website: www.epa.gov

The US Environmental Protection Agency is an independent executive agency of the US federal government that is responsible for matters related to environmental protection. It was established in 1970. Its goals include promoting environmental stewardship in policies regarding natural resources, human health, economic growth, energy, transportation, agriculture, industry, and international trade.

Good On You
Studio 1, Level 1, 2-12 Foveaux St., Surry Hills, NSW 2010
Australia
email: info@goodonyou.eco
website: www.goodonyou.eco

Good On You is a free app that helps consumers make better decisions on ethical shopping. It focuses on promoting the UN Sustainable Development Goals by compiling data on over 2,000 clothing brands gathered from the brand's reported data, certification schemes such as Fair Trade and Global Organic Textile Standard, and investigations by NGOs such as Greenpeace.

Intergovernmental Panel on Climate Change (IPCC)
c/o World Meteorological Organization
7 bis Avenue de la Paix, CP 2300, CH-1211 Geneva 2
Switzerland
phone: +41-22-730-8208-54-84
email: ipcc-sec@wmo.int
website: www.ipcc.ch

The Intergovernmental Panel on Climate Change is the UN body for assessing the science related to climate change. The World Meteorological Organization and the UNEP established it in 1988. Its mission is to provide policymakers with regular scientific assessments on climate change, its implications and potential future risks, and potential options for adaptation and mitigation.

Natural Resources Defense Council (NRDC)
40 West 20th Street, 11th floor, New York, NY 10011
phone: (212) 727-2700
email: nrdcinfo@nrdc.org
website: www.nrdc.org

The Natural Resources Defense Council is an international nonprofit environmental advocacy organization. It was founded in 1970 and has over 3 million members worldwide. It works to support clean energy jobs, fight climate change, and protect natural environments.

New Dream

PO Box 797, Charlottesville, VA 22902
email: newdream@newdream.org
website: www.newdream.org

New Dream is a nonprofit organization that promotes sustainability through working with individuals and communities to counter commercialism and overconsumption. It aims to help individual consumers make decisions that align with ecological, social, and community values. New Dream aims to change behaviors and social norms to reduce consumption and waste, offering resources to help encourage these changes.

Organisation for Economic Cooperation and Development (OECD)

2 rue André Pascal, 75775 Paris Cedex 16
France
phone: +33-1-45-24-82-00
email: angel.alonso@oecd.org
website: www.oecd.org

The OECD is an international organization that works with governments, policymakers, and citizens to shape policies that promote prosperity and address social, economic, and environmental challenges. It was founded in 1961 and has thirty-seven member states. It has created various reports and resources to help countries design and implement effective policies to address environmental protection and the sustainable use of resources.

Rainforest Alliance

125 Broad Street, 9th Floor, New York, NY 10004
phone: (212) 677-1900
email: info@ra.org
website: www.ra.org

Rainforest Alliance is an international nongovernmental organization that combines the interests of companies, farmers, foresters, communities, and consumers to produce sustainable goods. It was founded in 1987 and operates in over sixty countries. It awards environmental certification to businesses for sustainable forestry, sustainable agriculture, and sustainable tourism based on certain standards they have established and provides information to consumers about business practices.

United Nations Environment Programme (UNEP)
United Nations Avenue, Gigiri, PO Box 30553, 00100 Nairobi
Kenya
phone: +254 (0)20-762-1234
email: unep-newsdesk@un.org
website: www.unenvironment.org

The United Nations Environment Programme coordinates the UN's environmental activities and aids developing countries in adopting environmentally sustainable policies and practices. It was founded in 1972 and maintains a commitment to sustainability in its work as a global leader of environmentalism. In 2015 UNEP published its "17 Sustainable Development Goals," which it aims to enact by 2030 in order to address inequality and environmental challenges.

World Fair Trade Organization (WFTO)
Godfried Bomansstraat 8-3, 4203 WR Culemborg
The Netherlands
email: info@wfto.com
website: www.wfto.com

The World Fair Trade Organization is a global community of enterprises that fully adhere to the fair trade movement. The organization features an international "guarantee system" that ensures all member enterprises practice fair trade. It supports businesses around the world that promote ethical labor and environmentally sustainable practices.

Bibliography

Books

Ariana Agrios, ed. *Fair Trade* (Current Controversies). New York, NY: Greenhaven Publishing, 2020.

Jen Chillingsworth. *Live Green: 52 Steps for a More Sustainable Life*. London, UK: Quadrille, 2019.

Maurie J. Cohen, Halina Szejnwald Brown, and Philip J. Vergragt, eds. *Social Change and the Coming of Post-Consumer Society*. Abingdon, UK: Routledge, 2017.

Greta Eagan. *Wear No Evil: How to Change the World With Your Wardrobe*. Philadelphia, PA: Running Press, 2014.

Christiana Figueres and Tom Rivett-Carnac. *The Future We Choose: Surviving the Climate Crisis*. New York, NY: Alfred A. Knopf, 2020.

Jason Hickel. *Less Is More: How Degrowth Will Save the World*. London, UK: Penguin Random House, 2020.

Kathryn Kellogg. *101 Ways to Go Zero Waste*. New York, NY: The Countryman Press, 2019.

Naomi Klein. *This Changes Everything: Capitalism vs. The Climate*. New York, NY: Simon & Schuster, 2014.

William McDonough and Michael Braungart. *The Upcycle: Beyond Sustainability—Designing for Abundance*. New York, NY: North Point Press, 2013.

Adam Minter. *Secondhand: Travels in the New Global Garage Sale*. New York, NY: Bloomsbury, 2019.

Kathryn Roberts, ed. *The Economics of Clean Energy* (Current Controversies). New York, NY: Greenhaven Publishing, 2019.

Jeffrey D. Sachs. *The Age of Sustainable Development*. New York, NY: Columbia University Press, 2015.

Tatiana Schlossberg. *Inconspicuous Consumption: The Environmental Impact You Don't Know You Have*. New York, NY: Grand Central Publishing, 2019.

Dongyong Zhang, Stephen Morse, and Uma Kambhampati. *Sustainable Development and Corporate Social Responsibility*. Abingdon, UK: Routledge, 2018.

Periodicals and Internet Sources

Emily Atkin, "Does Your Box of 'Ugly' Produce Really Help the Planet? Or Hurt It?" *New Republic*, January 11, 2019. https://newrepublic.com/article/152596/hungry-harvest-box-ugly-produce-help-planet-or-hurt-it.

Ronald Bailey, "Is Economic Growth Environmentally Sustainable?" *Reason*, December 16, 2016. https://reason.com/2016/12/16/is-economic-growth-environmentally-sust1/.

Jeremy Butman, "Against 'Sustainability,'" *New York Times*, August 8, 2016. https://www.nytimes.com/2016/08/08/opinion/against-sustainability.html.

Eleanor Cummins, "Fast Furniture Is an Environmental Fiasco," *New Republic*, January 14, 2020. https://newrepublic.com/article/156208/fast-furniture-environmental-fiasco.

Sarah Friedmann, "Can One Person Make a Difference with Climate Change? Experts Insist Your Voice Matters," *Bustle*, September 16, 2019. https://www.bustle.com/p/can-one-person-make-a-difference-with-climate-change-experts-insist-your-voice-matters-18687241.

Maria Godoy, "Is a Diet That's Healthy for Us Also Healthy for the Planet? Most of the Time, Yes," NPR, October 28, 2019. https://www.npr.org/sections/

thesalt/2019/10/28/774205027/is-a-diet-thats-healthy-for-us-also-better-for-the-planet-most-of-the-time-yes.

Allison Hirschlag, "Can Secondhand Shopping Dent Fast Fashion's Environmental Damage?" *Scientific American*, November 7, 2019. https://www.scientificamerican.com/article/can-secondhand-shopping-dent-fast-fashions-environmental-damage/.

Sarah McFarlane, "Governments Eye a Green Economic Recovery. Some Industries Aren't Convinced," *Wall Street Journal*, July 7, 2020. https://www.wsj.com/articles/governments-eye-a-green-economic-recovery-some-industries-arent-convinced-11594113028.

Fred Pearce, "Local People Preserve the Environment Better than Governments," *New Scientist*, July 30, 2014. https://www.newscientist.com/article/mg22329802-900-local-people-preserve-the-environment-better-than-governments/.

Dean Snyder and Matt Guardino, "The Green New Deal and the New Politics of Consumption," *Jacobin*, March 21, 2020. https://www.jacobinmag.com/2020/03/green-new-deal-politics-consumption.

John D. Stoll, "Sustainability Was Corporate America's Buzzword. This Crisis Changes That," *Wall Street Journal*, May 1, 2020. https://www.wsj.com/articles/sustainability-was-corporate-americas-buzzword-this-crisis-changes-that-11588352181.

Laura Sullivan, "How Big Oil Misled the Public into Believing Plastic Would Be Recycled," NPR, September 11, 2020. https://www.npr.org/2020/09/11/897692090/how-big-oil-misled-the-public-into-believing-plastic-would-be-recycled.

Daniel Yergin, "The New Geopolitics of Energy," *Wall Street Journal*, September 11, 2020. https://www.wsj.com/articles/the-new-geopolitics-of-energy-11599836521.

Index

A

Adidas, 84
Alcoa, 74
Alexander, Samuel, 173–178
Amazon, 135, 171
American Action Forum,
      143–149
Anderson, Kevin, 65
ANZ, 85
Apple, 54, 94, 135
Ardern, Jacinda, 187
aviation, emissions caused by,
      22, 23, 38–40
Axelrod, Joshua, 48–52

B

Baekeland, Leo, 152
Bakelite, 152, 157
Bank of America, 76, 79
Batkins, Sam, 143–149
Bazilchuk, Nancy, 29–33
Bhasin, Lalit, 140–142
Biogen, 85
BMW, 85
Boeing, 135, 137
Borunda, Alejandra, 34–37
Boulding, Kenneth, 63
Bows, Alice, 65
Boyd, David, 115
BP, 53, 55, 61
Broadstock, David, 96–98

Brooks, 81
Brown-Forman, 75
Bruch, Carl, 116
Brune, Michael, 54
Byskov, Morten Fibieger,
      60–62

C

Canyon Creek Cabinet
      Company, 169
carbon dioxide emissions,
      causes of, 19–28
Carling, Joan, 117
Chan, Ryan, 169
Chevron, 53, 54–55, 61
China, 15, 29, 31, 35, 42–43,
      61, 121, 124, 130–131
climate change, 15, 23, 34–37,
      38, 39, 40, 41, 45–47, 48–52,
      53–55, 60–62, 64, 65, 73,
      74, 75, 90–92, 93–95, 115,
      118–134, 137, 165, 167,
      188–189
Coca-Cola, 74, 82, 85, 87, 93,
      94, 171
Commoner, Barry, 158, 160
Confino, Jo, 73–77
Cummis, Cynthia, 92

D

deforestation, 19, 20, 24–25, 189

degrowth, 17, 65–66, 174–178, 179–182, 183–187
Dell, 77, 79
Demaria, Federico, 63–66

E

ecolabels, 16
economic growth, sustainability of, 63–66
Enel, 91
Exelon, 75
ExxonMobil, 53, 55, 61

F

Facebook, 54, 135, 137
Faria, Pedro, 53, 54, 91
Fibre2Fashion, 68–72
Food and Agriculture Organization of the United Nations, 104–114
Ford Motor Company, 16, 74
fossil fuels, 19–28, 32, 35, 53–54, 61, 65, 127, 151, 155, 160, 166, 167
Freinkel, Susan, 153
Fromm, Sara, 184, 185, 186

G

General Electric, 74
General Mills, 76
Gleeson, Brendan, 184, 185, 186, 187
Google, 54, 79, 135
Goulder, Lawrence H., 118–134

Great Pacific Garbage Patch, 154
greenhouse gas emissions, 14–15, 16, 21, 24, 29, 31, 32, 38, 41–42, 48–52, 53–59, 61, 65, 73, 74, 75, 76, 91, 92, 102, 118–119, 120, 124, 131
greenwashing, 16

H

Haanaes, Knut, 84–89
H&M, 85, 91
Hewlett Packard, 83
Honda, 80
household consumption, emissions directly attributed to, 41–42, 43
Hyatt, John Wesley, 151–152

I

IKEA, 54, 85, 87
India, 35, 42, 46, 117, 121, 124, 140–142
indirect emissions, 23, 42
Intergovernmental Panel on Climate Change, 36, 115, 119
Ivanova, Diana, 29–30, 31, 32, 33

J

Jackson, Tim, 66, 182
Johnson & Johnson, 76

K

Kimberly-Clark, 50–51
Kolstad, Charles D., 118–134
Kronick, Charlie, 55
Kruschwitz, Nina, 93, 95
Kukreja, Rinkesh, 78–83

L

Legendre, Juliette, 179–182
Levermann, Anders, 45–47
Long, Xianling, 118–134

M

Mansholt, Sicco, 66
Mason, Matthew, 161–167
McDonald's, 78
Monsanto House of the
    Future, 156, 157, 160
Moodie, Alison, 90–92
Msuya, Joyce, 116

N

Nestlé, 84–85, 87, 91
Nike, 74, 84, 87, 93, 94
Novo Nordisk, 85
NRG Energy Inc., 91
Nunn, Ryan, 118–134

O

O'Donnell, Jimmy, 118–134
Ostrom, Elinor and Vincent,
    135–139

P

Paris Agreement, 15, 122, 189
Pepsico, 74, 85
Perryer, Sophie, 183–187
PG&E, 75
Pilling, David, 180
plastics, 14, 15, 16, 26, 50, 69,
    151–155, 156–160
polycentric governance,
    136–137
Pratt & Whitney, 82–83
Procter and Gamble, 49–51,
    77

R

Rauch, Joseph, 168–172
recycling, 15, 16, 51, 64, 70,
    77, 79, 81, 82, 83, 102, 154,
    155, 160, 164, 165, 169,
    171, 177
renewable energy/resources,
    16, 54–55, 62, 65, 73, 76,
    77, 79, 80, 83, 127–128,
    145, 161, 164, 167, 176,
    189
Riley, Tess, 53–59
Romero-Lankao, Patricia, 37

S

Science History Institute,
    151–155
S.C. Johnson, 81
Shackelford, Scott, 135–139
Shambaugh, Jay, 118–134

Shell, 53, 54, 61
Siemens, 87
single-use plastics, 16, 154, 156, 159–160
Southern Designs, 171
Starbucks, 75, 82
steady-state economy, 173, 174, 177, 178
Steiner, Achim, 188
Strasser, Susan, 156–160
Sustainable Development Goals (SDGs), UN, 165, 188–189
sustainable public procurement, 102

T

Taiebat, Morteza, 41–44
Target, 83
Telenor, 87
Tesco, 81
Tesla Motors, 16, 79–80
Toyota, 82, 85, 86–87
transportation, emissions caused by, 20–21, 22–23, 36, 37, 41, 42, 43–44, 62, 76–77, 80, 155, 169

U

Unilever, 84–85, 86
United/Continental Airlines, 80–81

United Nations Development Programme (UNDP), 188–189
United Nations Environment Programme (UNEP), 100–103, 115–117
universal basic income (UBI), 185–186

V

van der Heijden, Jeroen, 36
Victor, Peter, 66
Volvo, 54

W

Walmart, 16, 76–77, 80, 85
Watts, Mark, 34–35, 37
Westlake, Steve, 38–40
Westpac, 85
What's Your Impact, 19–28
Winston, Andrew, 93–95

X

Xu, Ming, 41–44
Xylem, 75